AF395713

By Ro-Ro
to the Baltic

Barry Mitchell

ISBN: 978-1-326-45428-9

Copyright © 2016 Barry Mitchell

All rights reserved, including the right to reproduce this book, or portions thereof in any form. No part of this text may be reproduced, transmitted, downloaded, decompiled, reverse engineered or stored in any form or introduced into any information storage and retrieval system, in any form or by any means, whether electronic or mechanical without the express written permission of the author.

Original narration published by Hutton Press 1985 as
Ro-Ro to Finland.

Published by Lodge Books 2014
25 South Back Lane
Bridlington YO16 4EY
www.lodgebooks.co.uk

Revised and updated 2016

Back cover illustration from a watercolour 'The Baltic Enterprise' by G. F. Overton.

Contents

About the Author

Barry Mitchell was born and educated in West Yorkshire. While serving in the Royal Air Force as a Radar Operator during the height of the Cold War he spent three years at an outlying underground base located on the Yorkshire Coast. Onwards he settled in the seaside town of Bridlington being employed at a local engraving business allied to the printing industry.

Having combined writing and hiking coastal paths as a pastime Barry Mitchell wrote articles about the area for regional magazines. Never far from the sea and ships, his writings soon included material of a nautical nature. The arrival of roll-on roll-off freight ferries became a draw to which this current tome is dedicated. Equally the growth of the passenger ferry services out of Hull saw him compile three successive books covering the progression of North Sea Ferries before the company became fully integrated within the P&O Ferries group.

Over a number of years Barry Mitchell has made sea crossings to all of the Scandinavian countries in pursuit of his hobby; likewise he has travelled to the near Continent on innumerable occasions aboard the NSF vessels. In retirement he continues his maritime interests appropriately living within sight and sound of the North Sea.

Introduction

Today's shipping industry faces constant economic challenges. Amidst the many financial pressures is the need to engage the most effective cargo handling systems that will subsequently increase the speed with which a waiting ship can be discharged, reloaded and put back to sea – the theory being that ships are too costly to be kept still.

This situation was equally prevalent several decades past. The ever increasing tempo of life in the post-war era had placed demands for increased speed and efficiency on all modes of transport. Consequently, the arrival of the roll-on roll-off principle of freight handling in the early 1970s was a revelation for the shipping industry. The system required a new breed of ship far removed from the conventional freight vessels of that time. As a result the dedicated roll-on roll-off freight ferry, or the ro-ro as it became more economically known, was born. Its conception, derived from World War II landing craft and early drive-on car ferries, enabled an entire shipment of freight to be loaded onto low-level wheeled trailers and hauled aboard in a space of hours where previously it had taken days.

The development of the ro-ro system was so radical that its basics remain little changed today, however the ensuing years have seen shipboard technology race ahead, eliminating seagoing jobs and skills that were once regarded as indispensable. Furthermore the economic climate behind the operation of a 21st century ro-ro ship is more challenging than ever – a situation requiring vessels to carry twice the freight volume than their trailblazing predecessors yet operating with almost half the number of crew. As such few, if any, short-sea dedicated freight ferries of today carry passengers other than road transport drivers who are adapted to self-service meals in unpretentious surroundings on single night crossings.

Ro-ro ships have always been somewhat elusive to the landsman: adhering to stringent sailing schedules the ro-ro spends but a few hours in turnround; in addition the berths that they use are under strict security and often physically remote from the public. Other than those professionally involved, few people ever have the chance to take a look at these vessels let alone to have the opportunity to step aboard and sense the mood of urgency under which they operate.

Back in the 1970s I had the good fortune of travelling as a passenger/reporter aboard the *Baltic Enterprise* in the mid-period of the ship's relentless ten years of UK/Finland voyaging. She was one of five Finnish-built 'Antares' class ro-ro ships which, at that time, were regarded as state-of-the-art in seagoing transport. The *Baltic Enterprise*, owned by the London-based United Baltic Corporation, was committed to a weekly roll-on roll-off freight service out of Hull marketed as Finanglia Ferries. She carried up to twelve passengers in more than comfortable, modern, Scandinavian-styled accommodation amidst an astute all-British crew of twenty-six skilled seamen. These were the days before GPS navigation, the internet, digital cameras, mobile phones or onboard smoking bans; days before unmanned engine rooms and before crew members were subject to a drinks prohibition. From a passenger's point of view, travel aboard that early generation of ro-ro ship was a blend of past traditions set against a background of a hard pressed ship being held to tight schedules through the competence of its officers and crew.

In keeping with the expected lifespan of a hard worked freight ferry, none of the 'Antares' class ro-ros escaped the passage of time. The opening years of the 21st century not only saw the closure of the United Baltic Corporation, but also the former *Baltic Enterprise* and her classic sister ships were unceremoniously despatched to the breaker's yard. Indeed over the years, that has been the eventual fate of all the ships mentioned in the text of this book.

Gladly my narration perpetuates the realism of voyaging aboard the *Baltic Enterprise* during the early years of the dedicated freight ferry. Here my ten day, late summer, Baltic voyage, sailing from Hull to four Finnish ports, was taken in an era of opposed political borders and wavering industrial progress; a time of the Cold War and the infancy of the European Union. In this respect it was a time long before the Baltic and its 'Capitals' became commonplace on cruise ship itineraries. The voyage is one of many scenic and historical highlights together with a background of sailing during a spell of temperamental weather – a feature of our northern climate that never changes!

Consequently the pages of 'By Ro–Ro to the Baltic' take the reader aboard a bygone, class-leading vessel and individually introduce its crew, on an intriguing, near three thousand mile round voyage of several decades past.

Barry Mitchell

Note. Prior to 1982 the internal vehicle/freight space on all roll-on roll-off ferries was not included in the measurement of the vessel's gross tonnage. Consequently, matched against present day shipping statistics, the gross tonnage of the pre-1982 ferries mentioned in this book deceptively undervalues their actual size. By example – later in her career the 1973-built 4,667gt. *Baltic Enterprise* was measured under the present day rules and subsequently re-registered at 12,110gt.
See page 168.

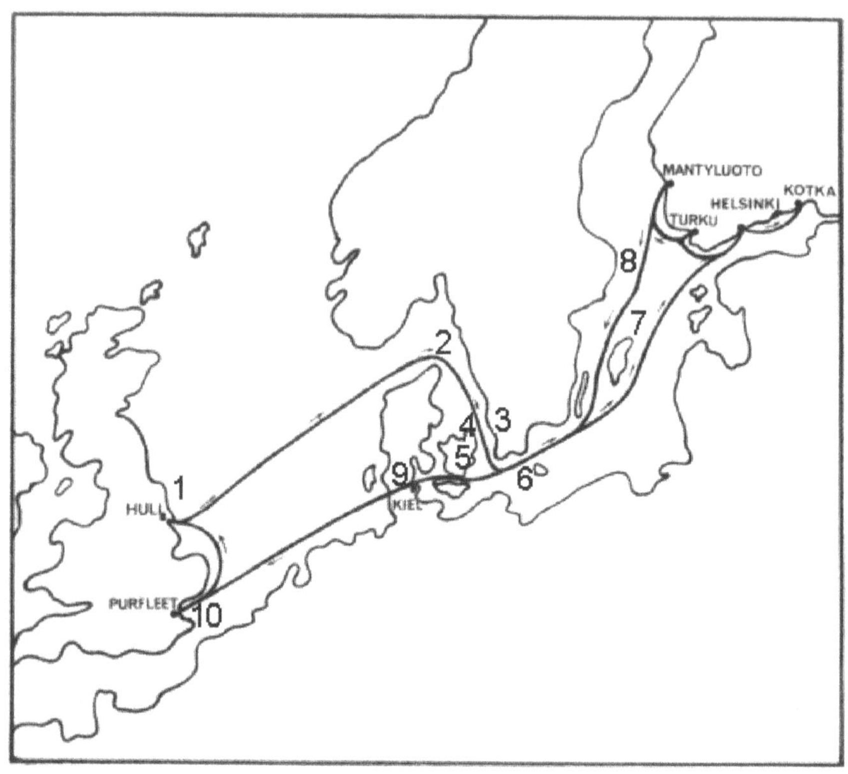

On completion of the eleven day round voyage the Baltic Enterprise had sailed 2,900 nautical miles. Along with the names of ports of call en route other strategic landmarks are waymarked thus:-

1	Spurn Point & River Humber (U.K.)		6	Bornholm (Denmark)
2	Skagen & The Skaw (Denmark)		7	Gotland (Sweden)
3	Helsingborg (Sweden)		8	Åland Islands (Finland)
4	Helsingor (Denmark)		9	Kiel Canal & River Elbe (W.Germany)
5	Copenhagen (Denmark)		10	Sunk Lightship (U.K.)

1. The Port of Hull, UK - August 1979

With radar aerials energetically rotating, flags tugging at their halyards and a plume of black smoke lifting from her hot funnel the *Baltic Enterprise* was in no way attempting to conceal the fact that she was a ship about to put to sea. The massive doors at her stern, which throughout the day had formed a horizontal bridge for an incessant perambulation of freight, were secured bolt upright. Towering surprisingly high above her aft deck they had transformed her hull into an impregnable fortress. The sheen from their grey-painted shell gently reflected the orange sunlight back westwards across a now deserted concrete loading ramp.

Apart from the six bar-taut mooring lines that spreadeagled downwards from her main deck fairleads the ship had severed all physical contact with the shore. Deceptively dwarfed by the great high-rise slab of her starboard side, the men who attend the quayside mooring bollards were last in line of a small army of people who had toiled throughout the day's oppressive heat to effect the ship's turnround. The clamour that had engulfed the vessel during that operation had subsided to a faint whisper – closed were the doors of the surrounding transit sheds, gone was the train unitised freight that had flowed from them, garaged was the vehicular apparatus that had relentlessly chugged and groaned to feed it into the ship's hungry belly. Remaining evidence of the dismissed procession was confined to tell-tale batches of refuse that lay around a dusty dockside.

This cessation of waterside activity marked the prelude to a late summer weekend which for those ashore held the promise of a couple of relaxed work free days. But for the *Baltic Enterprise* and her crew it marked the commencement of another chapter in an encyclopaedia of voyages between the shores of Britain and Finland.

Measuring 4,667 gross tons *Enterprise* was one of the dedicated roll-on roll-off freight ferries that had become known in the shipping world as ro-ros. Owned by the London-based United Baltic Corporation she operated together with sister ship *Baltic Progress* on a specialised 'high-speed' UK/Finland service. Two further identical vessels of the five ship 'Antares' class, *Orion* and *Sirius,* owned by the Finland Steamship Company of Helsinki, were also involved. The combined operation was a partnership of the two companies known as Oy Finanglia Ferries Ltd.

The 4,667 gt. *Baltic Enterprise* entered service on the Finanglia Ferries UK / Finland operation soon after delivery from her Finnish builders in March 1973. (G Robinson.)

The *Baltic Enterprise*'s latest homeward voyage had terminated at the Humber port of Hull in the early hours of that morning. Having discharged 4,000 tons of unitised freight before midday she had reloaded with an equal capacity of British exports in readiness for the scheduled 19.00 departure to Helsinki. Now, with main engines running, she was waiting her turn to enter the lock that would facilitate her release from the Queen Elizabeth Dock to the River Humber.

Aboard her, I had entered an environment of pile carpets and plush seating; a world of sophisticated electronic instruments and modest professionalism, of lavish meals and technically biased conversation, of containers, trailers, lashing chains and engines. The mood generated there was that which a small self-contained community adopts while in the throes of briefly detaching itself from the turmoil of landward life.

Presiding over the lock pit entrance at that very time was the North Sea Ferries', Rotterdam bound *Norland*. Many of her passengers thronged the decks to witness the skills of her master in coaxing her 12,988gt mass through the lock's open jaws. For several moments, as the ferry angled in the breeze, doubts would be raised as to the feasibility of the exercise. However, with variable pitch screws churning a maelstrom of brown water to check her sideways momentum, the largest Hull-registered ship crawled forward until, with barely nine inches clearance at either side, she was encompassed within the grey walls. Some eight miles downriver was one of the *Norland's* smaller fleet-mates – *Norwind*. She had negotiated the lock thirty minutes earlier and was by then stemming the Humber flood tide towards the open sea and her morning goal – Zeebrugge. Since inaugurating their services with one ship in 1965, North Sea Ferries had invested prudently to create an each direction, seven days a week, motorway to Europe operation.

At the time of completion in June 1974 the 12,988gt *Norland* was regarded as the world's largest passenger ferry. She is seen here prepared for her overnight Hull/Europoort crossing.

Ferries like these had paved the way for the ro-ro principle to become an accepted means of handling general cargo. It was realised that the facility of high-speed turnrounds was becoming an essential factor in the economics of short-sea operations. Thus in the early 70s many conventional freighters were phased out in favour of the cargo-on-wheels system. In a profession where old traditions die hard the ro-ro ship had raised unanimous applause. They had not only brought shipboard comforts to a standard unimagined only a couple of decades previously, but also a whole new lifestyle to those who crewed them.

While pondering at *Enterprise's* bridge wing it seemed fitting that I should be commencing a voyage aboard the new generation of ship at Hull. Being traditionally a seaman's town it had borne the wind of change that for seven hundred years had persistently blown across its waterside. Consequently the waters that confronted me circumscribed the present maritime element there and also reflected the traumatic days gone by.

Though there is evidence that Hull existed more than one hundred years earlier, it is generally accepted that Edward I was the founder in 1293. During a hunting holiday in the area he was invited to inspect a growing port that was situated at the confluence of the River Hull with the Humber. Being impressed with what he saw he named it Kings Town upon Hull.

Over the following centuries Hull, as it became more economically called, has had periods of vast development and prosperity together with times of dire hardship and depression. Not least of Hull's problems came in the twentieth century, for in World War I German submarines continually hampered Humber shipping while at the same time airships bombed the docks and town. Unfortunately that was only a foretaste of things yet to come, for twenty-one years later Hull was this time one of the main targets of the German Luftwaffe. Throughout the heavy bombardment of World War II, the enemy had to remain in ignorance of the damage they were inflicting on the port so it was only after the hostilities had ceased that anything could be published about it.

In the recovery years after the war Hull's deep-sea fishing industry was at its peak – the commercial docks were equally thronged. Then the situation completely reversed itself. International political sanctions totally decimated Hull's future as a fishing port and, at the same juncture, where commercial shipping used to be a lifeblood of Hull it progressively dwindled to become an integral segment of its varied industrial assets. Hull's condensed shipping activities then being concentrated on the deep-water King George and Queen Elizabeth Docks which broach the north bank of the Humber three miles east of the city centre.

Two hours earlier my journey to Hull had terminated at Queen Elizabeth Dock. There, far overreaching a substantial transit shed, the 1973 Finnish-built *Baltic Enterprise* was berthed at No. 15 Quay. Before boarding, a vista of the ship had priority so, enjoying the warmth of the summer day, I walked the dockside to take in her vital statistics. Soon I was in a position to establish that, like most ships, the *Baltic Enterprise* was at her visual best when viewed at an angle to the bow. Here the overall impact was size. Her modest sounding tonnage suggested a relatively small vessel, but gazing up at the U.B.C. logo crowning her towering forepeak one could have been excused for taking her for a ship in excess of 12,000 gross tons.

Flaring aftwards from her bow, raising to the height of a house from the water with a minimal amount of sheer and being totally unbroken by portholes, the formidable walls of her hull created a striking impression of bulk. In silhouette from the opposite shore *Enterprise* could have been seen as a scaled-down tanker or bulk carrier, for her main superstructure sited almost aft was somewhat characteristic of that of the giants that ply between the oil terminals of the world. Agreed, most of her lines were either horizontal or perpendicular. She decidedly lacked the graceful contours familiar in tonnage of yesteryear but, in fairness, the innumerable multi-coloured containers that were continually being stacked along the expanse of her weather deck were steadily contributing to her angular appearance. The very essence of unit load transportation is in the squaring-off of each freight unit; result – containers. In submission to the proverb 'You can't fit a square peg into a round hole', angular cargoes require angular ships to transport them!

When seen at the Finanglia terminal, Hull, the *Baltic Enterprise* and her 'Antares' class sister ships give a perspective of appreciable bulk.

It is unlikely that any ro-ro vessel could have been more purpose built than the 'Antares' class ships. Yet in retaining the main superstructure towards the after end the marine architects had happily upheld a basic traditional image. By displaying a squat cream-painted funnel *Enterprise* scored well against many of her contemporaries – here, reed-like uptake exhausts poking from the extremities of a ship's quarters had become the rule rather than the exception. Equally, to her advantage, neither did her gleaming white superstructure rise like a city tower block; its stepped sides, furnished with orange lifeboats, were progressively flanked with wide orchard green decks. In summary, considering she was a pure ro-ro freighter, the *Baltic Enterprise* outwardly displayed a certain distinctive styling. Whether it was this unpretentious, yet individualistic appearance or otherwise simply because I was aware that the vessel was to be my mentor for the next nine days, I did not know, but the more I contemplated her, the more favourably I looked on her functional lines.

While the building of a vessel of this class during the early 1970s involved an investment of £10 million the day-to-day operating costs were equally phenomenal. Fuel, insurance, maintenance, food, pilotage and harbour dues combined to evoke overheads that would stagger the man in the street. Not surprisingly ships are operated on the principle that they are too costly to be kept still. Every hour spent idle whilst waiting a berth or wasted in the handling of difficult cargoes weighs heavily on the debit side of the balance sheet. On this account the age of the unit load arrived more as an economic necessity than as a novel mode of sea transportation. In this respect, where a conventional freighter employed on short-sea trading could spend upwards of 60% of the year at the dockside, a ro-ro ship on the same trade would not be expected to be immobile for more than 25% of the year.

During an earlier visit to Hull these facts were made clear to me by the U.B.C. Port Captain Chris Woodall. On that occasion I was shown over two conventional U.B.C. freighters. Fresh from dry dock the *Baltic Venture* was about to be loaded with general cargo for the Polish port of Gdynia while on the opposite quay, sitting on her load line with 3,400 tons aboard, the *Baltic Valiant* was ready to depart on her regular service to Leningrad. I was told that the *Valiant* had arrived from the Russian port similarly burdened nine days earlier. The lengthy turnround had resulted from the handling and stowing of myriad items of individual freight. Related to a ro-ro system the vessel could have been heading back to sea with the same amount of freight within twelve hours.

"In principle the ro-ro system allows the ship's deck to be prepared in the transit sheds before turnround day," Woodall explained. "All items of freight – textiles, building materials, feeding stuffs, machinery, fertilisers or vehicle parts for example – are pre-loaded onto slave trailers or into containers before the ship arrives. On berthing it's 'all systems go', first unlashing the incoming loaded trailers from the ship's decks, hauling them ashore to the intake bays then reversing the procedure with the export freight."

Working around the *Baltic Enterprise* that hot August day were eighteen dockers and fourteen riggers. Their labours of driving and securing aboard the 3,800 tons of outward freight was the culmination of three day's work involving some sixty employees at the Hull base of the Finanglia operation. At the quayside amidst the fervour, the lithe bearded figure of Chris Woodall was much in evidence. Directing the loading operation was a job that kept him on the move; on foot, bicycle or further afield in a white estate car that displayed the Finanglia logo.

Eventually I was able to pin him down to renew our acquaintance –
even then our meeting was brief. The reverberating noise of the
chugging Tugmasters made conversation uphill work but in all, I
gathered that he was more than satisfied with the turnround.

"So far things have run quite smoothly – no labour problems,
breakdowns or bad weather – another hour should see the job
completed," he shouted.

At a safe distance I watched the two hundred horsepower Tugmaster
vehicles haul trailer after trailer aboard the ship. Each load was
individually driven onto one of the 'tween decks which were accessed
through the stern doors. On entering the hollow, cathedral-like interior,
traffic for the upper 'tween deck was elevated by means of an internal
ramp and parked on one of the six lanes that were marked out along the
length of the ship. Additionally at this level two hatches allowed
containers to be lifted from their trailers and deposited on the outside
weather deck above. This was effected by a 23-ton gantry crane that was
driven on tracks forward of the superstructure. When the internal ramps
were reversed access was gained to the lower hold that had
approximately half of the capacity of one of the 'tween decks. Together
the four freight decks provided space for 288 twenty-foot units with
room to spare for a variety of vehicles such as lorries, tractors, cars or
caravans. The loading process was fascinating to watch. From my
vantage point it seemed that no matter how many units were 'rolled'
aboard, the ship consumed them without any undue congestion.

It was time to go aboard. Passing the ro-ro's starboard quarter, which
was embellished at the rim with large black lettering bearing BALTIC
ENTERPRISE LONDON, I made my approach. Way beneath, the
calibration at the waterline showed that she was drawing over nineteen
feet – adding my meagre twelve stones aboard was not going to change
that!

Double stacked containers being loaded onto the ship's lower 'tween deck.

Twin stern doors formed a double bridge allowing simultaneous loading/unloading.

2. What! No Tugs?

A regular tourist would compare the accommodation area of the five Antares class ro-ros to that of a small, Scandinavian influenced, three star graded hotel. Being enclosed within the main superstructure it raised three decks from the main hull section. It was a completely independent unit comprising every up to the minute amenity necessary to comfortably accommodate both crew and up to twelve passengers. In providing this no corners had been cut; on first entering the accommodation block one reacted to a smartness and quality above and beyond all expectations.

The 'hotel manager' aboard the *Baltic Enterprise* held the rank of Catering Officer. He was directly responsible to the Captain for the day-to-day administration of the accommodation and catering requirements for all those aboard. Apart from handling catering accounts, ordering stores and provisions, supervising stewards and pantry boys, together with the welfare of passengers, he was regarded as a father figure within his section. Aboard the *Baltic Enterprise* the catering officer image was amicably portrayed in the ample figure of John Garvey. In his late forties he was a man who had sailed to almost every corner of the world on ships as varied as the countries he had visited. The last sixteen years of his seagoing career had been spent with the U.B.C. company.

On approaching the ship's stern I had been met by a young, fair haired officer who had identified me as one of seven passengers due to embark for the imminent voyage. From there on, my guide had taken me upwards through the ship's innards to a veneered door on the second level of the accommodation area. Here, in the Catering Office, John Garvey extended a warm welcome to the ship and having dealt with my travel documents gave me a brief tour of the public areas of the accommodation. We were soon recalled to his office to meet an expected pre-departure visitor to his department – the duty Immigration Officer.

Becoming adjusted to my new surroundings I found that my luggage had been placed on a rack in one of the two forward facing, generously sized passenger cabins, a seat awaited me at the centre table in the dining saloon, and a quick introduction was made to several of the ship's company who were dashing away to their respective stations.

My first meal aboard was a hurried occasion with the imminent departure taking preferential interest over what appeared to be a well-balanced menu of traditional British food. Everyone seemed to have somewhere to go or something to do; consequently it was not long before I joined the exodus from the U.B.C. inscribed tableware. I had been invited to the bridge – moreover to witness *Baltic Enterprise* manoeuvred from her berth, through the lock pit, and piloted the twenty-two miles down river to the North Sea. Therefore the tightly sprung door at the head of a short inside stairway that led upwards from the main accommodation area was my objective.

BAGGAGE

– Passengers paying full fare are allowed to carry baggage consisting of their own personal effects to the extent of 1 cubic metre, and children in proportion to the amount of passage money paid for them. The shipment of any quantity *in excess* of this allowance will be charged for as follows:–

Baggage must consist of personal effects only. Household equipment, furniture and crated items etc. will only be accepted as freight.

Passengers are recommended to insure against the risks of loss of life, personal injury and illness and against loss of or damage to luggage and effects and to ensure that the terms of their Motor Insurance Policies are extended to fully cover their vehicles whilst in transit by sea including the process of loading and unloading as well as for foreign travel.

UNITED BALTIC CORPORATION LTD   MACANDREWS & CO LTD

24-26 BALTIC STREET, LONDON EC1V 0TB TEL: 01-253 3456 TELEX: 269783

Entering the bridgehouse I was confronted with a spread of consoles massed with banks of multi-coloured switches, knobs, dials and levers creating a scene that could have been taken from a scaled down space centre. They lined two thirds the width of the silent interior beneath nine angled windows that overlooked the weather deck twenty-five feet below. To the rear of this scrupulously tidy control room was a screened-off area containing chart tables, chronometers, drawers and desks where entries into the ship's log were made. Directly in the centre, rising from the carpeted deck, was a plinth shouldering the rudder direction indicator, the gyro compass display, together with the ship's wheel – not really a wheel, a small semi-circular helm similar to those seen in an aircraft cockpit.

The Bridgehouse M.V. *Baltic Enterprise*. The ship's wheel is located at the plinth seen on the left.

Latched to it were the hands of a swarthy able seaman who, waiting for orders, stood reverently with eyes firmly glued to the instruments before him. At each end of the fifty-five foot wide bridgehouse was a lavishly varnished sliding door that provided access to the open bridge wings that crept outwards to overlook the ship's sides.

Assembled on the starboard wing were: the master of the *Baltic Enterprise,* Captain Gerald Brazendale – he was in his mid-forties, stockily built and had a good head of hair that tended to fall over his forehead; the ship's Chief Officer, Peter Green, who was a lean six-footer of thirty years of age; and finally Humber Pilot John Ashby, a man in his late forties who was content in taking a back seat until the ship was manipulated to the river.

While peering over the side the Captain was issuing orders through a portable radio telephone that was strapped to his shoulder. In response to his commands, fore and aft mooring deck crews, who had been called to their stations earlier, began to winch aboard the heavy warps that one by one were being loosened from the quayside bollards by shore hands.

Hands hovering over the engine controls, Captain Brazendale craned his head back and forth calmly waiting for the moment the ship would be totally detached from the wharf.

An important characteristic of a ro-ro freighter is that under normal weather conditions it is equipped to manoeuvre in and out of port without assistance of tugs. This has been arranged by dispensing with the age-old telegraph system between bridge and engine room. Instead, the Master has direct control over the engines both from the main fascia in the bridgehouse and duplicate controls sited at the extremities of each bridge wing. These neat, twin (inverted 'L' shaped) levers not only govern the amount of power transmitted to the propellers but also control the amount of pitch inclined upon them. For range of pitch and power each lever is calibrated through an arc from zero to ten both ahead and astern.

A further and most essential innovation towards independent handling is the bow thrust propeller. Set deep in the water at right angles to the hull this electrically driven screw can be operated at variable speeds either to port or starboard, effectually giving the provision of a small tug working at the bows.

Within the confines of Hull's Queen Elizabeth Dock, the *Baltic Enterprise* appeared a ship of considerable size – this, few would dispute. The exercise of taking her safely from the Finanglia Terminal, through the lock pit and onto the Humber tideway was entirely dependent upon the expertise of the Master in the handling of the engine controls and in his calculated commands to the seaman at the wheel. Motioning Chief Officer Peter Green to his side, Brazendale nonchalantly brought in the starboard engine to three ahead. Meanwhile Green hung on to a button below the white side coaming to effect a long bellowing siren blast that panicked countless gulls from the dock waters. Gradually one could detect a snail's pace forward motion.

Enterprise had been moored starboard side to the quay with her stern firmly butted against the wide concrete ramp. Ahead, slightly angled across her bow at No. 14 berth, lay a conventional freighter of around 5,000gt. There were approximately seventy-five feet of clear water between the two vessels. The lock basin was directly astern, sited at ninety degrees to the ro-ro berth. In the exercise of presenting her bows to the lock jaws she had to be pulled away from the quay for several yards in a crabwise manner. This created sufficient clearance for the stern to be swung out at forty-five degrees. Situated thus there was enough clear water to enable her to be taken astern around three ship's lengths – turning tightly a further forty-five degrees to starboard to give a direct heading into the lock.

The R.T. squawked out a message from Second Officer Bernard Elworthy on the aft mooring deck, that there was enough clearance astern of the ramp for the ship to be pulled away. Brazendale worked at the controls – three astern starboard engine, four ahead port engine and bow thrust half speed to starboard – and expectantly returned his gaze to the quay edge. Hesitantly the forward crawl ceased giving way to a detectable sideways motion that opened up a moat between ship and shore.

The process of manoeuvring the burdened ro-ro from its berth to the open sea for this voyage was a ritual of persuasion by a team of twelve men – four on the bridge, six manning the fore and aft mooring decks and two deep down in the engine room watching over the banks of dials and gauges that issued performance readings from the entanglement of thudding machinery down there.

The Captain's cautious moves had been orchestrated as a tentative measure because, pushing against the port side, a fresh evening breeze was tending to hold the ship against the quay heading. Having tested her stride against this encumbrance he whisked the controls into a wider gait – six astern starboard, six ahead port and bow thrust at full to starboard. In almost immediate response to this directive the ship awoke from a leisurely attitude into a burst of energy. Stirring one's eardrums the funnel-top exhaust broke from a relaxed murmuring into a heavy rhythmic bark thrusting skywards a volley of soot-speckled clouds. Deep down, the large screws, opposing each other in the laborious task of drawing the laden ship from the staging, bit furiously at the brown water inducing bouts of quavering vibration to dissipate through the hull. Widening, the moat became a river – a river of swirling, opaque liquid escaping from a seething cauldron beneath the stern.

"When we have a wind of over force five in this direction we have to call for a tug to give a helping hand," Brazendale called over to me as I watched him open the respective engine controls to eight in each direction and cutting the bow thrust. Keeping a low profile while the

Captain concentrated on the ship's progress I gave a cursory acknowledgement to his statement. Later I was to learn that when the wind reaches that strength swirling across the dock a great deal of turbulence is stirred up. Apart from the windage on the ship's side, freak eddies are created resulting in the ship being able to move but a few yards from the quay then being held there.

"Hard to starboard!" Brazendale called in full voice.

"Hard to starboard!" came the customary response from the steersman at the wheel.

With the stern swinging out with increasing speed, Peter Green sited himself on the port wing to act as blind side lookout. There was little doubt, judging from the satisfaction shown on Brazendale's face, that the manoeuvre was going strictly to plan.

Remaining unobtrusive during this process, Pilot Ashby paced to and fro across the wing duck boarding, firstly watching the action from the rail and then the bridgehouse, intermittently glancing at his wristwatch obviously calculating the state of the tide. Although the pilot is in charge of the vessel from the time it has been cast-off until it reaches the river mouth, it is accepted that on a ro-ro ship the captain will conduct the close manoeuvring within the dock. It is not expected of anyone to jump into the driving seat of a vehicle he does not handle on a regular basis and manipulate it with the dexterity of one who is well practised.

Drawing his attention I questioned John Ashby on this point. "All conventional ships have to use tugs to take them to the river," he explained. "The pilot always takes full control of that operation. With ro-ro ships things are a little different – each has its own whims which require time to master. Usually the captain prefers to take the controls and we have no objection to this arrangement," he added. "The one exception is in the case of Russian ro-ros. Surprisingly all masters of these ships ask the pilot to handle the whole operation. Normally one or two arrive here weekly from Leningrad delivering U.K. destined Lada cars, so we are not entirely without ro-ro driving experience!"

Scanning the now empty berth, our bow momentarily pointed at Chris Woodall, arms folded and leaning against his car. The U.B.C. Port Captain had finally adopted a stationary posture to watch the ship make its exit. For him it was the wind up to a hectic week and the start of a two day break. Come Monday the Finnish ship *Sirius* would be arriving to occupy the berth and every minute of his time.

Of the four identical ro-ros operating on the Finanglia Ferries services, two, *Baltic Enterprise* and *Sirius*, sailed on a regular basis out of Hull. One ship covered the south coast of Finland, first calling at the capital, Helsinki, and then on to Kotka – an industrial centre some ninety miles to the east. The other ship made for the west coast of Finland, taking in Turku, a major shipbuilding centre and ferry port, and then moved a hundred miles north to a remote port with a far-sounding name – Mäntyluoto.

Of the other two vessels the *Baltic Progress* maintained a regular seven day service out of Purfleet, on the north bank of the Thames, to Helsinki while the *Orion* held sailings out of Felixstowe every Friday to Turku and Kotka.

To all intents we were departing on the Hull – South Finland service. However there was to be an interesting diversion on the return voyage. At that particular time sister ship *Baltic Progress* was undergoing her annual dry docking, this leaving her capital to capital run to be temporarily covered for ten days by her fleet mates. Consequently, while on our scheduled call at Helsinki we were to take aboard some Purfleet-bound freight. On completing our Finnish loading at Kotka the re-routing was to take us through the Kiel Canal directly to the Purfleet base. On return from the Thames to Hull we would have sailed close on three thousand miles, half of which would be close by the shorelines of five different countries.

The lock pit into which we headed to commence that journey served both King George and Queen Elizabeth docks. It was opened in 1914 to accommodate ships of up to 750 feet in length and 85 feet beam. Having secondary gates approximately one third of the way along its length, the water capacity can be greatly reduced, allowing smaller ships to be worked through more quickly. After the *Norland* had been lowered to the river, the outer gates had been closed, the pit re-flooded and the inner gates opened for our entrance. The operation of sluicing the lock into the river had little or no effect on the ninety acres of dock it served. A nearby pumphouse ducted to the river is geared to feed back and maintain a constant level.

From high up on the bridge, as our ship nudged between the stone piers, the ship appeared to be wider than the distance across the pit. However, when foot by foot our Captain edged her between the yawning inner gates, the illusion subsided. In concentric movements he would turn to scan along the hull checking against any deviation in the parallel run to the piers. Seventy-three feet away, Peter Green in likewise manner was keeping the same vigil over the port wing. Then in response to what seemed an inaudible message through a V.H.F. speaker, Pilot Ashby broke off a quiet verbal exchange with Brazendale to move into the bridgehouse. There, dark glasses pushed onto his forehead, the uniformed Pilot issued a progress report through a hand microphone to the controller at the Spurn Pilot Station. Meanwhile, retaining his fixed stare at the rudder direction indicator, the seaman at the wheel seemed totally oblivious to this intrusion of the bridgehouse quiet.

Ships taking their leave have always attracted a variety of onlookers. Often they are relatives or loved ones of those aboard. Some are there purely to satisfy their own curiosity, yet others are sentimentalists to whom the occasion holds an irresistible magnetism. Few though they were at the lock side that summer evening the ship gazers there seemed to fit into such groups. And to them, with her battleship grey hull and ice-cake superstructure tinged with the flame of the deepening sun, the *Baltic Enterprise* must have presented a formidable sight.

Perhaps some would see her as a snorting, lumbering, burdened workhorse, though anxious to be reunited with her own element after a twelve-hour rest, reluctant to be penned through a narrow corral before being released. Certainly there were noises to back up that vision. First, as the Captain thrust her bow a foot or so one way and braked the move with a dash of adverse power, they would hear the intermittent bursts of clanging vibrations from the head of the oncoming beast. Then as the main bulk advanced there would be the incessant roar of breathing from the fresh-air ventilators sited midway along the accommodation block. Further, and foremost, as the master cracked the whip on the main engines to check the eager animal's drift, growls of contempt would echo from the sky-high funnel top. Augmenting these volleys of pulsating sound from that elevated voice box was the perpetual low thud from the very lifeblood of the brute – its generators. In reality they did see a 460-foot long ro-ro freight ferry bedecked with steel containers coaxed smoothly into the King George Dock lock pit.

The capacity to manoeuvre a 460' freight ship in and out of port without tug assistance was one of many beneficial innovations that arrived with the ro-ro era. (Ken Lubi.)

Twenty-five minutes had passed from leaving the ro-ro berth to the shore hands catching the heaving lines thrown by the deck crews and hauling the weighty mooring warps over the white-topped bollards at the lock side. Having barely an hour left to run, the flood tide had reduced the drop to the river to eight feet. Anyone who had walked to the lock head at that time would see a ten minute cascade of boiling turbulence as this differential of water was released through the submerged sluices.

Those who had stood back purely to see the ship that had arrived and was descending before them would notice it was far from devoid of human habitation. There were men busying themselves both fore and aft. Six passengers were leaning on the boat deck rails. Above were three uniformed figures in conference on the overhanging bridge wing – a seventh passenger, who had been stood with them, was now on the highest part of the superstructure scanning the Humber environs through binoculars.

Not that I expected to find wildlife above the bridgehouse, but I did agree with Peter Green's statement that I would find that the 'monkey island' was the ultimate vantage point aboard ship. Superseded in height only by the buff-painted steel mast and the black rim of the funnel-top, the 'monkey island' was the uppermost tier of the ship's superstructure. Flanked by waist high, rail-topped coamings its broad green acreage was uninhabited save for a number of strategically placed navigational aids. On deep sea voyaging this outpost could be used for taking sightings from celestial bodies, but on that occasion the vantage was that I had an unrestricted 360 degrees vista of Humberside.

By this time *Baltic Enterprise* was being slowly lowered to the river level. Astern, countless common gulls darted to and fro before eventually settling on the rippled lake of dock water. Beyond, from that high platform, the skyline revealed the outer fringes of East Hull with its stretches of flat open country, dotted here and there with high-rise flats and industrial complexes. Westwards, partially silhouetted by falling sunlight, the starboard side faced an urban backcloth which was the heart of the city. Standing out over the rooftops was the slender wafer building of the Royal Infirmary, whilst the tower of the 13th century Holy Trinity Church was a feature near the riverside. The church is in the Old Town where other buildings prominent in Hull's history are in abundance – The Guildhall, Trinity House, Wilberforce House and the Old Corn Exchange to name but a few. Not the least of the many curiosities there is a lane named 'Land of Green Ginger'.

Then there was the huge river highway in a summertime disguise of shimmering silver. Being two miles wide at that point the Humber has gathered great strength. A glance at the map of northern England reveals how this river gains that power. This estimated 5,000-mile river system, that drains one fifth of the country, is often described by taking the Humber as a right forearm with a hand containing some nine fingers. These tributaries having a bold assortment of intriguing names – Swale, Ure, Wharfe, Aire, Calder, Don, Derwent and Rye – flow together to form the palm, the River Ouse. Gaining even further prosperity from the Rivers Trent and Hull, the Humber surges from the wrist onwards to the sea and claims the distinction of being Britain's greatest watershed.

Upstream, through the glasses, I could see at a distance of eight miles the construction site of what would become the Humber's crowning glory. On completion the Humber Bridge would boast a span of 4,626 feet between its 525 feet concrete towers, its total length between the Humber shorelines was to be 1.25 miles.

Walking over to the port side rail our height advantage over the nearby transit sheds allowed a clear view of the Saltend Jetties where two small, rust-streaked tankers were berthed for the purpose of discharging at the nearby B.P. refinery. Again, accentuated by the low-lying land that broached its shores, the main impact here was the ever-widening River Humber. I began to consider the voyage ahead and remembered that on this occasion the familiar stretch of water before me was the prelude to a cruise across the North Sea, the Kattegat, the Baltic Sea and in three days time the Gulf of Finland.

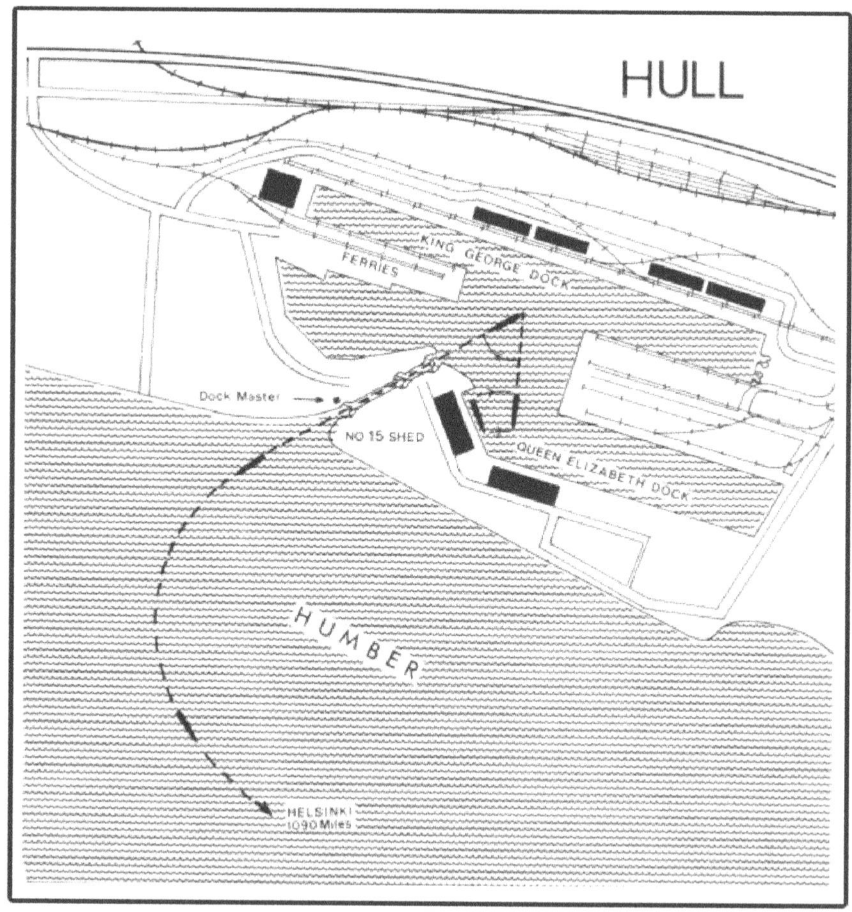

3. Seaward Pilotage

Looking beyond the neat lines of deck cargo, the squat steel foremast and the curvature of the ship's white bulwarks, the way had been opened up to the river. Though I had failed to notice the outer lock gates fold parallel with the grey masonry of the lock pit I could not miss the strong blast from the ship's siren as we crept towards the Humber fairway. Below me the two master mariners continued to direct operations from the starboard bridge wing – Captain Brazendale still handling the engine controls while Ashby scanned the river from the forward protective coamings.

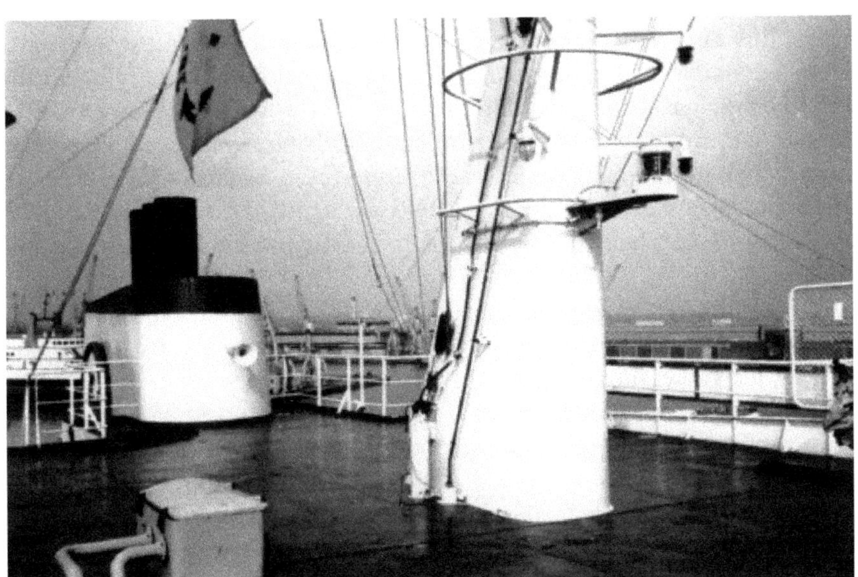
Being the topmost deck the spacious Monkey Island gave an all-round vista.

The encounters between masters and pilots are brief. There is seldom any social connection to divert their conversation away from the job in hand. They meet purely on business and, since the pilot normally boards the ship within minutes of the scheduled departure time, any social prelude is generally limited to a handshake over the captain's office desk prior to going to the bridge. Replacing the lack of personal friendship is a secure professional etiquette that each strives to respect. In doing so, they unite a wealth of nautical expertise to guide a ship safely across uncertain waters. On this occasion, Brazendale was the authority over the uncertain moods of a burdened freight ferry, Ashby the delegated skill over the fickle whims of the Humber.

Down on the extremity of the lock pier the Dock Master, a formidable, white-capped figure, transfixed his eyes on the moving steel walls. When finally the ship's stern doors came clearly into his view he issued the all-clear by means of a long shrill note from his pocket whistle. Now, free of the dock constraints, the *Baltic Enterprise* was in position to be brought into a tight port turn of some 100 degrees against the flood tide onto a seaward heading.

"Hard to port!" Brazendale rasped from the wing.

"Hard to port," echoed back from the shaded interior.

In this situation the effect of the bow thruster was most apparent. Here a conventional general cargo freighter would rely heavily on a lead tug to bring her head round into the tideway. But with the bow propeller thrusting at full power to starboard, starboard engine at seven ahead and port engine pulled back to six astern, *Enterprise* reacted with a show of independence. Heeling a degree or two to starboard, as her bow scoured the distant south bank shore, she made short work finding the direction of the salt air.

"Midships!" During the turn Brazendale had shifted his control position to the bridgehouse. Now, no longer necessary to bellow the orders, his voice, though quieter, still revealed a sharp edge.

"Midships," retorted the man at the wheel.

Standing at the main engine control fascia the Captain turned to Ashby, "Rudder midships and making seven knots Pilot." He had set the ship on the broad river fairway, bows headed towards the sea and making more than amble steerageway. Obviously this was the signal for Ashby to take over.

John Ashby was a man of cheery disposition. He took over with a bounce of self-confidence.

"Thank you Captain, one-three-five please."

"One-three-five steady."

Leaning forward with arms spread against the shining consoles, the Pilot carefully matched *Enterprise*'s idle progress to the dial readings before him. The seven knots recorded there was of course the speed that we were travelling through the water and not relative to the land. With the last of the tide still producing a two knot current against us the land seemed to linger abeam.

"I think we can make that ten knots, Captain."

Gerry Brazendale acknowledged and hastened to make the adjustments through the neat levers on the dias.

Out on the port wing, away from the atmosphere marked with dextrous control, the pace was more definable. *Baltic Enterprise* was beginning to collect herself, pushing dark wedges of murky water scornfully away from her towering hull. The Pilot was steering us along the deep-water channel that initially held to the north bank of the Humber. The steady forward motion had turned the evening air decidedly cooler, and with every yard we travelled one could anticipate the awaiting tang of the sea. In this sedate attitude *Enterprise* seemed to have regained a certain dignity that ships lose when bound to the quay of a harbour or dock. This imagined contentment could be detected through the audible change in her attendant noises drifting over the stern. It could be felt in the gentle vibrations through her rails. It could be seen as the black, soot-filled exhaust gave way to a blur of hot grey air from the funnel top.

Once away from port the normal shipboard routine of watch-keeping settles down. In this respect watch-keeping aboard *Baltic Enterprise* naturally conformed to standard international practice. Besides the Master, who under normal conditions did not stand watch, she carried the accepted minimum of three watch-keeping navigating officers. Likewise, the engineering section was made up of three watch-keeping officers who were directly responsible to the Chief Engineer. These six men stood watches of one four-hour period in every twelve. Consequently each man had two spells of duty every day spent at sea in this rotation:-

	BRIDGE	**ENGINE ROOM**
00.01–04.00	Second Officer	Third Engineer
04.00–08.00	Chief Officer	Second Engineer
08.00–12.00	Third Officer	Fourth Engineer
12.00–16.00	Second Officer	Third Engineer
16.00–20.00	Chief Officer	Second Engineer
20.00–00.01	Third Officer	Fourth Engineer

Completing the ship's complement of eleven officers were three non-watchkeepers: the Electrical Officer, who was attached to the engineering section; the Radio Officer, who had fixed hours of manning by day and, being accommodated adjacent to the radio room, was on twenty-four hour standby; and finally, the Catering Officer whose busy daytime routine I had already seen. Other ranks of registered seamen, greasers, cooks and stewards made up the ship's total complement of twenty-six men.

With two miles of the Humber behind and twenty ahead I was joined at the rail by Peter Green who had been relieved from watch by Third Officer Willie Maclaughlan. Our departure time had coincided with Green's watch. Now off duty he was destined for a relaxing hour in the Officers' Smoke Room before turning in for an early night.

Shortly after leaving Hull the riverside village of Paull was seen from the ship's port side.

Though the distance between ship and shore was steadily widening the squat white tower of Paull Lighthouse at the waterfront village of that name looked only a stone's throw away. It was constructed in 1836 when the Brethren of Trinity House deemed the necessity of a navigational light on that stretch of shore. No longer used, it was sold and converted into a unique private residence commanding unrivalled views of river traffic. A half mile downstream of Paull we passed a small shipyard. Surprisingly in the days of decline in both fishing and shipbuilding industries it was kept busy constructing middle distance trawlers.

A sudden change in exhaust tempo announced that more had been called of the engines. They struck up in unison to promote a bold harmonious thunder that gripped the after decks. A distinct pulse from underfoot augmented this businesslike proclamation. As the Chief Officer and I walked aft along the wide, green-painted deck the effect of the increased power was more than evident. *Baltic Enterprise* had awakened from her muted stride to produce a traumatic influence on the Humber tideway. A succession of white-topped curling waves splayed with fervour from her sheer sides. Twenty feet beneath the surface the thrashing propellers ejected a watery meringue that spread astern twice the width of the ship.

"That will be ten ahead both engines – probably seventeen knots," Peter Green informed me above the exhaust noise. He was to add that until we were out on the open sea the engines were normally governed back to 80% of full power. Despite the application of 'full ahead' we were running under the usual service speed. "Once clear of the Humber we ask the engine room for 90% power. This will give us around eighteen to nineteen knots."

The Humber vista from the aft rail was unreal. Almost at its full height the tide had swallowed the mud banks and saltings that are all too familiar to those who frequent that unpredictable waterway. Disguised in the glow of a low fiery sun the murky expanse of the Humber and its normally dull shores took on semblance of a faraway riviera.

While we marvelled at that rare scene, Bo'sun Peter Edwards appeared on the deck below. He unceremoniously lowered the Red Ensign that throughout the day had been fluttering at a tall staff that angled aft from the rails beneath us. The large flag that Edwards carefully folded was normally flown while the ship was in port. At sea a smaller version of this flag was flown, together with the house flag, from the mainmast from sunrise to sunset. Among a host of duties for which he is directly responsible to the Chief Officer, the Bo'sun and his men spend much of the daytime painting the upper structure of the ship.

Seizing the opportunity of a quick progress report from his subordinate, Green quietly excused himself and was away down the steel stairway.

Ten miles out of Hull the deep-water channel closed in on the south bank. There, an unpopulated marshy shoreline had given way to a vast complex of industrial development. First were the Killingholme Oil Terminal jetties. Here our pilot brightly asked for a reduction in speed. Brazendale obliged by halving our headway into the tide. This adjustment was accompanied by the sound of released air pressure from beneath the console – a noise not unlike that issued from brakes of a commercial vehicle, but less characteristic was the rate of deceleration; it was barely detectable.

Between calling for course alterations, first five degrees one way and then the other, Ashby talked about pilotage of supertankers on the Humber, for it was alongside these south bank jetties that the true giants of the ocean discharged crude oil from the Arabian Gulf. Seemingly the larger vessels of this class arrive after discharging half of their cargoes at Rotterdam. In this situation they can be drawing forty to fifty feet of water and berth at Immingham less than a mile downstream from Killingholme.

To avoid having to embark the Humber pilot ten miles out to sea it had become practice for the pilot to take the ferry overnight to Rotterdam. Having enjoyed the outward voyage as a passenger he would then return in the same capacity on the tanker before commencing duties at the ten mile approach to the Humber. This was an amicable arrangement for both pilot and ship's master alike. It can take several miles and up to twenty-five minutes to slow a 250,000dwt tanker from its usual sixteen knots to a suitable pick-up speed. Here the master is happy to have the pilot aboard and avoid stopping in a strange, crowded and relatively shallow seaway.

Added to the physical problems that evolve through such a manoeuvre the time factor can also be a crucial element. Like ro-ro ships, and sometimes even more so, supertankers are subject to stringent timetables. Dire efforts have sometimes been made by their masters to adhere to them. This has been highlighted through unfortunate disasters that have occurred where, in cutting a corner to save a few miles and precious minutes, tanker masters have put their ships on the rocks.

Every stage of a tanker's turnround is scrupulously programmed. Even the half hour taken in stopping to board a pilot and getting underway again could mean missing a tide in a few weeks time at the other side of the world. Maritime regulations covering 'Rules of the Road' had been extensively revised to give supertankers the right of way in restricted waters. To claim this priority they have to show certain lights and give advanced warning of their approach.

Disappointingly on that Friday evening the tanker berths at both Killingholme and Immingham stood empty and unattended. There was however much else on the south bank to catch the eye. Hereabouts, while holding a gentle pace, we passed the entrance to Immingham Dock. This, being the Humber's busiest port, was in the 1970s handling a greater volume of cargo than that of Liverpool and Hull combined. Whereas Hull gained its impetus as a port during the 17th, 18th and 19th centuries, Immingham attained its rapid growth in the 20th century through the development of the large steelworks at nearby Scunthorpe.

The bridge of our ship provided the elevation to afford a useful view of the area. Certainly the metropolis of deep-sea ships, oil storage units, cranes, sheds and office blocks would contrive a scene far removed from the Immingham Creek that the Pilgrim Fathers knew in 1608. It was from here that they originally set sail before crossing the Atlantic in 1620. Street names in the nearby village of South Killingholme commemorate that occasion.

Here my thoughts sprang back to another original voyage from there; the occasion being a memorable first-time sea voyage to the continent for my wife and I aboard Tor Line's sparkling new 7,042gt *Tor Anglia* in 1967. Part of Tor Line's inauguration programme was the operation of fully inclusive, wintertime mini-cruises between Immingham and Amsterdam, departing Friday evenings to return the following Sunday morning. This was an outstanding introduction to ferry travel for us at an unbelievable low cost – £8 per head!

After the 1967 arrival of sister ship *Tor Hollandia* a two-way triangular service between Sweden, Holland and England was fully commenced. In 1975 the success of the route led to the building of impressive new ships: the 15,794gt *Tor Britannia* and *Tor Scandinavia*. On their arrival the UK passenger terminal was relocated to Felixstowe.

When new in 1966 the 7,042gt. *Tor Anglia* opened a 'triangular' passenger/freight service that linked Immingham, Gothenburg and Amsterdam. Tor Line's success resulted in the 1975 building of larger vessels. In consequence the UK terminal was moved to Felixstowe.

With Immingham astern, *Baltic Enterprise* continued seaward along the broad lane of buoys and marks that she had obediently followed from her berth. Because the river current is often running fast and strong many of the Humber marks were set upon double-ended, flushed-decked steel boats that give every appearance of scaled-down lightships. Under such conditions conventional buoys can become deceptive, primarily through straining at the limit of their moorings and adopting a horizontal attitude.

Occasionally the Pilot would point out buoys and marks named after the sands they guard – Clay Huts, Holm Hook, Burcom and Clee Ness – others had just been re-sited because of ever-shifting sand and mud banks. "The Humber charts require constant updating to accommodate these changes," Ashby said.

Although regulations demand that a pilot should be engaged to navigate ships upwards of 1,500gt on such waters, it is the master who shoulders ultimate responsibility should anything go wrong. If a master suspects that his ship is being steered into danger, though not commonplace, he is at liberty to override the pilot's instructions. The probability of such happenings aboard the *Baltic Enterprise* that evening seemed as remote as the stars that were beginning to peep through the darkening backcloth. Temporarily dispossessed of his command, Brazendale appeared totally relaxed by showing no indication of questioning the Pilot's judgement. Clearly contributing to this self-assurance was the way in which Ashby not only gave intelligible, decisive orders but offered a cheerful explanation of his actions to those who happened to be within earshot.

The Spurn Pilot Station from which the 150 registered Humber pilots operated had been labelled as the most modern of its kind around Britain's shores. Prior to its opening in 1976, duty pilots were based aboard the dated pilot cutter *William Fenton* which was moored in the lee of the Spurn headland. Sometimes, due to spells of bad weather, the inadequacy of that arrangement led to temporary closure of the service. The new shore station provided the pilots with sophisticated radar and communications systems; operating at a much higher degree of efficiency and at a fraction of the cost of building a new cutter. Alongside the six-tier control centre is a pier that extends 850 feet out into the Humber. This provides for a minimum depth of nine feet of water; therefore the pilot launches are fully operational at all states of the tide.

It is said that over the centuries, the Spurn peninsula has gradually risen from the sea through millions of tons of sand, gravel and boulder clay being swept down the Yorkshire coast. On meeting the fierce Humber current this wasted land matter has been thrown up to form a three-mile, finger-like ridge where little grows except coarse marram grass and a selection of wild flowers. In many places this narrow tract of land is no wider than the bumpy road that runs along its entire length. The road not only provides a landline for the pilots but is the principal link with civilisation for the small community of residents at the 'Point'; the neat row of simple cottages that nestles amid the dunes at Spurn were the homes of the Humber lifeboat men and their families. Due to its remoteness and the demands called upon it the Humber Lifeboat has the distinction of being the only R.N.L.I. craft to be manned by a full-time crew.

In common with all R.N.L.I. stations, the Humber has a long history of men who have fearlessly challenged the dangers of the sea. Not least of the Humber lifeboat luminaries being Coxswain Brian Bevan who, in 1979, was the first man in the 155-year history of the R.N.L.I. to be awarded the Gold, Silver and Bronze gallantry medals all at one time.

From our ship it was the beam of Spurn Lighthouse piercing the dusk that gave initial bearing of the headland. But shortly, with *Enterprise* scything away the remaining ten river miles, the Spurn peninsula rose from the horizon in the guise of a low undulating breakwater. To starboard the lofty one million brick hydraulic tower on the Grimsby waterfront had been the final landmark from the south bank. To all appearances we were now on an open seaway confronted only by a finger of land that reached down from an indefinable north bank. In the bridgehouse the shirt-sleeved Maclaughlan, unprompted by his superior, removed the daylight masks from the three radar consoles, resulting in the faces of the Captain and Pilot being warmed intermittently by a rich orange glow as, in turn, they wandered to and from the informative screens.

"090 – 085 – 095 – 105," were the commands given by Pilot John Ashby to guide the ship along a thread of twinkling navigation marks during the final miles of the river journey. He was busier now, not least in raising contact with the pilot launch which was to rendezvous with *Enterprise* to effect his departure. The launch, which surprisingly was blessed with my surname, *Mitchell*, was engaged with fleet mate *Fox* shifting pilots to and from a flotilla of ships riding at anchor around the river mouth.

For the earlier stages of our river passage we had only encountered the occasional coastal freighter making either for the wharfs of the River Trent or the 'inland' port of Goole that lies fifty miles upstream from the sea. For the latter stages the broad waterway became increasingly busy with a wide variety of merchant tonnage – coasters, tankers, a 40,000dwt ore carrier *Appleby*, conventional freighters and ro-ros aplenty.

An inference of the ro-ro era was spelled out clearly by the words FAST LINE emblazoned along the hull of an inbound freight ferry. It had become normal for shipping companies to use the towering sides of their vessels as advertising space; ro-ros and passenger ferries providing an obvious hoarding. Breaking that rule the U.B.C. ships were among the minority of short-sea traders that had, gladly, not taken advantage of this.

Soon we closed in on Spurn. Half a mile abeam of the port rail the ghost-like formation of the headland was spearheaded with the pilot station itself. This was a structure not unlike the control tower of a small airport. From its darkened windows the Pilot Master would be observing the solid form of our ship as we glided smartly by. Behind the pilot station the tall black and white banded lighthouse spread its warning at regular ten second intervals over river and sea. Over and beyond the buildings at the 'Point' the eerie form of the Spurn headland disappeared into a watery background.

Abruptly, a message from the pilot launch crackled from the console-mounted loudspeaker: "Mitchell to Baltic Enterprise, do you read me?"

"Baltic Enterprise – Mitchell – affirmative."

"Can make it in ten minutes, that okay?"

Ashby hesitated, momentarily scanned the sea lane ahead, then announced: "Sounds okay to me, see you in ten minutes – out."

At Spurn Lightship, four miles onwards, Captain Brazendale assumed full command of his ship. Following a last minute consultation and a firm handshake with Pilot Ashby, he immediately asserted his authority across the bridgehouse to both his subordinates remaining there. "Starboard five!" Then turning to Maclaughlan, in a quiet tone asked, "Will you escort the Pilot to the deck please?"

From the starboard wing I watched a high-speed launch race out of the gloom. Our ship was now at a subdued 'three ahead', welcoming the pilot craft alongside. Of strong business lines, these launches were built to the design of the 'Arun' class lifeboat. In the half light *Mitchell* heeled and bounced on the fickle water that had been aroused by the slowing ship. Dwarfed beneath *Enterprise*'s high-rise sides she was soon tucked in close and obscured from view to all except those who overhung the outer rails. Third Officer Willie Maclaughlan and the departing pilot were at the hatchway on the starboard side of the weather deck. From there a steel ladder led through the innards of the lower 'tween deck where a small pilot door had been opened. The last lap of the descent to the sea was by means of a short rope ladder that dangled vertically from this door over the ship's side.

Pacing between the bridgehouse and starboard wing, Captain Brazendale was intent on retarding his ship's pace to effect a smooth pickup yet holding sufficient steerage way.

"Starboard ten!"

The burley helmsman who in strong voice had promptly repeated the calls from both Master and Pilot on our river passage had been stood down to an older man whose narrow face was brought from the shadows by the gentle illumination from the compass rose.

"I called starboard ten, could you speak up please?" Brazendale, through the gentle swing of the bow, had detected the application of his order but not heard the customary response. His caustic tone of admonishment received an immediate reply.

"Starboard ten Captain."

"Steady as she goes!" Brazendale bellowed.

"Steady as she goes." Though troubled with a croaky voice, the new helmsman was more than anxious to reply.

John Ashby had wasted no time in descending to the launch. Clutching his small document case in one hand the Pilot laconically turned a glance skywards and waved into the big ship's searchlight with the other. Brazendale reciprocated in similar vein as he watched the gap between the two vessels widen.

For a time the bridgehouse atmosphere was much the poorer for the absence of Ashby. His lively banter and knowledgeable commentary were past. Rightly Brazendale and his Third Officer were fully involved in the business of clearing the coast and heading the ship towards Scandinavia.

Now that his presence was more meaningful the keen-eyed young Scotsman worked at fulfilling various mandatory functions. The correct charts had to be available at a second's notice while at the same table the ship's log had to be kept up to date.

"Full away at 21.51," Brazendale called in the direction of the illuminated table.

Then the internal phone buzzed with calls, resulting in two seamen walking out to the bow to 'secure anchors' and the watch-keeping engineer opening the main engine governors allowing 90% of maximum power.

The Captain switched *Enterprise* onto automatic pilot and promptly dismissed the seaman from the wheel. To starboard, only the lights of a group of ships at anchor or quietly making their way to the river mouth separated us from the wide ocean. The disposed helmsman was now posted to 'lookout' duties on the wing to keep a watchful eye over them. Maclaughlan joined the seaman at the rail. With an outstretched arm he scoured the blackened horizon indicating the lights which required a special watch.

Striking out for the Humber Lightship (10 nautical miles from the coast and the last staging post before the long reach to northern Denmark) the *Baltic Enterprise* settled on eighteen and a half knots, issuing no more than the gently 'lolloing' motion of a lake steamer. Astern, beyond our silver wake, the shore lights were being drawn away as though on invisible strings. One thousand and fifty nautical miles ahead a Helsinki ro-ro berth lay waiting. Above, the exhausts thundered their rhythmic bark into the night sky. Below, a cosy bar, a tray of sandwiches and a comfortable bed were signalling a welcome.

A pilot launch speeds away from Spurn Pilot Station at dusk. The station is situated at the point of the narrow three-mile long Spurn peninsula.

4. The Hospitable North Sea

Throughout the year as I head for work, my daily routine starts with a journey along the seafront. There are several routes that I could choose but my car seems automatically programmed in order that I can glimpse the horizon across the broad sweep of Bridlington Bay. Today, from the open deck of a modern ro-ro freight ferry on a course of 052 degrees, I also looked out at the horizon but, although it was the same sea, the view that normally confronted me was many horizons distant over our port quarter. The morning was superb and today I had time to linger.

We had moved on into Saturday in the company of a light westerly breeze and an endless succession of kindly faced waves. The sea had caught the mood of the sky and now two hundred miles of vivid blue water separated the *Baltic Enterprise* from Hull and the River Humber. On reflection I suppose anyone making for The Baltic in a lesser craft may not have looked upon those North Sea corrugations with such an easy mind. But gazing down upon them from the security of the high-riding weather deck one could be excused for taking their worth with total unconcern for, one after another, they submitted to the complete destruction offered by the racing bulk of our ship. As we bore down upon them in progressive slaughter the value of their resistance was smashed, churned and creamed into a bleached fairway of confused water that extended a mile and beyond astern. By way of a respectful gesture *Enterprise* had adopted a gentle 'roll'; this, opposed to the almost terra-firma-like stability we had experienced the previous evening, gave one a not unpleasant feeling of actually being at sea.

Walking out to the bow alongside the lofty lines of containers, I looked out on a sea devoid of shipping of any sizable significance. There were one or two motionless dots that I assumed to be working fishing vessels, that apart, nothing more than sea and sky.

Overnight our arrow-like course had carried us south of Dogger Bank. Peter Green had confirmed this when, on commencing my early morning constitutional, I had made a brisk visit to the bridge. The bank is an underwater shelf of sand extending 170 miles from north to south, and 60 miles from east to west. The least depth over the bank is 14 metres. For generations it has proved to be one of the North Sea's most lucrative fishing areas so it was hardly surprising that we should meet trawlers in the vicinity. However when the weather promises to cut rough the fishing fleets give Dogger Bank a wide berth.

"Big winds and 'short water' mean steep seas," a local fisherman once told me.

Peter Green too endorsed that statement by indicating that in severe conditions Dogger Bank was a place to be avoided by ships of any size.

On arrival at the forward mooring deck, I was in a three-cornered area enveloped on two sides by ranging solid bulwarks that splayed forward in unison to form the ship's rounded forepeak. Behind was a high wall of steel running athwart ships. This fortress not only formed a barrier between the weather deck cargo and mooring gear but acted as the foundation of the squat foremast. Hawsers and winches, anchor chains, hawse pipes and windlasses, this was the main furniture up front. Everything tidily secured into place, well greased and carefully painted. This wasn't gear designed only to take strain (which it did in large degrees); it had to take weather also. On such a day it was hard to envisage huge seas crashing over that high bow, but they did, and all the mechanism there had to survive and function afterwards.

The most striking feature about that lonely outpost was the feeling of detachment from the rest of the ship. This was chiefly brought about through the absence of any mechanical noise or vibration which, though we had been at sea but a modest twelve hours, one had subconsciously become adapted to. Not that life within the superstructure was furnished with perpetual teeth-chattering auscultation of pounding engines and juddering propellers – far from it. Yet the steady whisper from the air conditioning ducts in each room together with a defined underfoot vibration, with its attendant noises induced through the transmission of ten thousand, five hundred horsepower to the propellers, promoted an awareness of the driving force beneath.

So apparent was the transition from that aliveness to the blunt water-shedding sounds echoing upwards through the hawse pipes that the two places seemed to belong to separate worlds. The only indication of the power being exerted 150 yards abaft was the rolling cascade of seawater anxiously splaying away from the unstoppable grey bow. Standing there, excelling in the morning sunshine and salt-tinged air, I could for all intents have been on some remote headland overlooking a vast blue ocean to the distant tune of the moving tide.

There was a generous amount of deck space around the accommodation block at all levels.

On the after-deck things were different. Behind the accommodation block the vibrations were strong; to the extent of shaking the miscellany of steel fittings into a symphony of metallic crescendos. The broad area of green-painted deck was alive with an unseen force. This was a place of work. Again there were huge winches and, raised high above the stern rails, blocking any prospect of a view astern, were the upper sections of the stern doors. The electrical control mechanism for those massive blockades stood across the wide transom in the form of two shoulder-high, white-painted cabinets. Here also, a small crane that was used for hoisting stores aboard tremored above the starboard rail.

I wasn't the only person to be out and about at that early hour; there were men swilling the upper decks. This I discovered on narrowly avoiding a drenching from above. Bo'sun Edwards and his deck crew held this long brush and water cannon event each day. Particularly after leaving port, the exhausts blasted a rime of hot soot skywards. Some of this black grit deposited itself on the apple green decks of the after end. Without regular attention it would have been walked (much to the Catering Officer's dismay) onto the sacred, alleyway carpets.

The 'watch out below' shouts that saved me from an unscheduled shower came as I approached an opened superstructure door on the main deck. Emitting from that door was the exclusive aroma of grilled bacon. This obviously was the galley where two white-coated cooks moved industriously around a centre island stove. I did not enter to impede on their good work – breakfast was a priority!

There were times when the opposing tracts of crew and passengers were more evident than others, none more so than at breakfast time. Clearly this time of day was not the most opportune for social exchange between the two groups. As such some crew members may be just going on watch and others ready for bed rest after a trying early hour spell of duty. Spasmodic appearances were made, essentially by the more senior officers, but excluding the Captain whose breakfast tray was taken to his quarters. Escaping the fussing of white-jacketed stewards in the saloon, the other officers preferred their bacon and eggs in their less formal mess room one deck below.

Away from breakfast other mealtimes were a different call. This was the opportunity for engineers and navigators to meet face to face, in contrast to their distant telephone conversations between engine room and bridge; when 'Sparks' briefly descends from his high mission in the radio room; and when the Catering Officer breaks away from his stock and requisition sheets. During these fleeting get-togethers they talk shop. Whether it's a faulty valve in the engine room, an increase in freight rates or a medical course for senior officers, mealtimes provide the opportunity to air views. These were men in their working environment, individual members enrolled to sail the ship safely and to schedule. That was their job and that is what they talked about. Not that these men were being unsociable towards their paying guests – to the contrary, many is the time when an off-duty man has yarned long after the table has been cleared and the dishes racked.

Passengers aboard the Finanglia Ferries services usually fell into three specific groups – business people, holiday travellers and transport drivers. It is doubtful that any of these people expected or desired to be thrown into an extravaganza of shipboard entertainment by a wily cruise director – if they did they would be sadly disappointed! Regardless of their comfortable accommodation these were working ships, working under pressure. Hauling thousands of tons of freight around northern Europe was their bread and butter, passengers adding only the barest covering of jam.

Apart from myself, the ensemble of passengers who, after the 8am breakfast call had drifted into the dining saloon that Saturday morning, fitted snugly into the three categories. Bob and Ruth Turnbull were to travel alongside me for the round voyage. They had left a busy Birmingham retail business in the hands of their family to take two weeks of relaxation. They liked sea travel but could not stand crowds or regimentation – cruise ships were not on their agenda. They had travelled on conventional freighters on a number of short-sea voyages; this was their first taste of a ro-ro vessel.

Taking the opportunity of mixing a summertime business trip with a short Nordic holiday, David Jackson, accompanied by his wife Jean and teenage daughter Susan, would be driving his car off *Baltic Enterprise* on arrival at Helsinki on Monday afternoon. David had three calls to make in Finland on behalf of a large concern of precision tool manufacturers whom he represented. The family were then to move on to Sweden when, after further visits, they were to return to the U.K. via the Gothenburg-Newcastle ferry.

Transport drivers were not regular passengers on the Finanglia route; virtually all the freight carried was unaccompanied – on its own wheels, loaded onto 'Mafi' trailers or into containers. However I was told that from time to time *Enterprise* had carried vehicles as diverse as security vans, experimental buses, juggernaut excavators and racehorse boxes. On this crossing we had one such 'special' accompanied load. Philip Rowe was the driver of a furniture van that contained the household and business effects of a British family who had moved to central Finland. He had driven aboard at Hull after a four hour journey from Coventry. On arrival at Helsinki he faced a similar distance. In the meantime in his words it was to be, "Feet up and a good book."

M.V. BALTIC ENTERPRISE - PASSENGER INFORMATION

MEAL TIMES

MORNING TEA (on request)	07.30	Passenger Cabins
BREAKFAST	08.00-09.00	Dining Saloon
MORNING COFFEE	10.30-11.00	Passenger Lounge
LUNCH	12.00-13.00	Dining Saloon
AFTERNOON TEA	16.00	Passenger Lounge
DINNER	18.00-19.00	Dining Saloon
SUPPER	21.00	Passenger Lounge

Waiter service, all meals taken in the saloon – silver service at dinner.

*

As the morning wore on we continued to purr our way across the North Sea amid brilliant sunshine. For the passengers, deck chairs on the starboard bridge deck provided the greatest draw. Tactfully sheltered from the airy breeze created by the ship's incessant forward 'way', the chairs and loungers were lined up where the sun would flood down until late afternoon. The sunbathing ritual was occasionally broken by one of the participants surreptitiously rising and walking to the rail in anticipation of an oncoming ship or even the sight of land. There was no stampede when at such time a steward would arrive to announce that morning coffee was waiting in the passenger lounge or that the bar was open for lunchtime aperitifs. One by one the occupants of the chairs dragged themselves upright, slipped on a shirt or top and quietly, almost reluctantly, disappeared indoors.

For all that we were on the main Humber-Baltic route the sea was almost devoid of traffic. Over midday I had looked in at the bridge. It was watch changeover time; both Second and Third Officers were present. Their conversation was focused on a mid-sea obstruction which, on our heading of 052 degrees, we were steadily bearing down upon. The North Sea was splattered with exploratory gas and oil rigs or production platforms. One of these structures was directly ahead some seven miles distant. On taking over the bridge watch Second Officer Bernard Elworthy's initial task was to sidestep the ship to starboard allowing a comfortable clearance. His manipulation of the autopilot was perceptible to the ear in the form of a rapid but muted click-a-click-a-click. Gradually the ship edged over to the right until the pulsations from the autopilot suggested that the rudder was again being centralised.

I had recognised Bernard Elworthy as the young man who had courteously escorted me aboard the previous afternoon. He brightly explained, "By pushing her over just a few degrees at this distance it saves making a tighter turn at a closer range. Even so we will soon have plenty of clear water to comfortably give that monstrosity a wide berth."

As he spoke the inner bridgehouse door opened. Like any conscientious master, Gerry Brazendale was in the habit of making unscheduled appearances on his bridge. On this occasion I suspected that he had detected the slight change in course and automatically found himself checking the reason. Not that he showed mistrust in the actions of his Second Officer, and not that he was unaware of the presence of the rig for it had been obstructing the main lane for some months. Inwardly, Brazendale was a quiet family man with his roots firmly placed in the Dorset countryside. Six months of the year his profession placed him in a world alien to this domestic existence; up to thirty-eight people, ten million pounds worth of ro-ro ship and three million pounds worth of freight were his direct responsibility.

Elworthy did not come forward with explanations; he had no need to. The Captain knew that the ship had been steered carefully away from the obstruction. For the rest the chart told him all he wanted to know; we were on course and on time. With an air of satisfaction he ambled across the expanse of the bridgehouse carpet to join his Second Officer on the sundrenched starboard wing.

The North Sea is splattered with exploratory oil/gas platforms. The ship was side-stepped to starboard allowing a clear passage past one such structure on our outward journey. (FotoFlite.)

Mid-afternoon we were confronted with a fellow ro-ro freighter. Gleaming topsides and a broad, royal blue hull reflecting the brightness of the day, she gave the impression of a vessel new from the builders. I had been watching her from high on our 'monkey island' since she appeared from over the horizon but a few points to port. Tearing at an undecided sea that parted in a plume of sparkling white spray in varying measures on either side of her bow, she conveyed the unseen picture of our own ship's indulgence. Obviously, making a comparative speed to ourselves and being on a reciprocal heading of 232 degrees the distance between the ships was soon cut down.

Abeam she displayed an array of containers as variegated in colour and markings as those that filled our own weather deck. In this profile her identity was revealed. Without the aid of glasses the words TOR LINE emblazoned in white against her blue hull were more than readable; and when showing her port quarter (on which a group of seamen appeared busy on daily maintenance) TOR NERLANDIA LONDON was the announcement. Retracing our own steps back to the Humber I assumed her to be on the Gothenburg-Immingham route.

It was early evening before Denmark was sighted. Showered, changed and contemplating a drink before the 18.00hrs dinner call, David Jackson and I were at the aft rail marvelling at the flight pattern of a dozen or so gulls that effortlessly slipstreamed the ship. Wings outstretched with never a beat they swooped and lifted around the stern forever maintaining the ship's pace. At first the land appeared as an obscure image almost beyond the horizon down the starboard side. A further five miles of wake had spread astern before the haze presented itself as an endless frontage of undulating sand dunes.

To be specific this was the province of Jutland, the bulky part of Denmark that assumes a narrow, forty-five mile waistline at its border with Germany, that frontier being the only part of the country to be attached to the European mainland. Here and there, during our eighty mile run in company with the Jutland coastline, the continuity was broken with the sighting of villages that in summer provide a welcome retreat for business weary Danes. Beyond these small communities one could see little, for the agricultural landscape that covers 90% of Jutland raises barely above sea level; nowhere in Denmark does the land raise more than 483 feet above sea level, this point being Himmelbjerget (the Sky Mountain) in the Skanderborg region of Jutland.

Shortly after meeting the Danish coast Peter Green had changed our course to 065 degrees. This heading was to carry us to the northernmost tip of the country named The Skaw, which is something of a North Sea junction for ships on Scandinavian and Baltic routes. Incessantly holding her service speed *Enterprise* slowly, very slowly, overhauled an accompanying dank looking freighter on which, while alongside, one could pick out an unpronounceable Russian title and the hammer and sickle against her red-banded funnel.

It was about this time that that ship developed a more pronounced 'roll', apparently not an unexpected motion in those waters for even in the summertime the meeting point of the Skagerrak, Kattegat and North Sea has a reputation for getting 'ruffled'. It wasn't a vicious roll but for the first time one became conscious of the need for hand rails along the alleyways, in the stairs and around the decks.

Dinner went by in a holiday mood. Sun reddened faces, incessant chatter, bright summer prints and lightweight jackets were the passengers' contribution towards breaking the workaday atmosphere. The ship had suddenly become alive with noise and colour. With both on-duty, watch-keeping officers being briefly relieved for their evening meal, as many as sixteen people were seated at one time. Engineers, of whom little had been seen during the day, boosted the numbers. Excepting Chief Engineer Clive Buchan, who was a regular 'patron' of the dining saloon, the watch-keeping engineers found it unpractical to change from working suits to meet the dress code of the saloon every mealtime. Dinner was the exception and they arrived uniformed, as their fellow navigators, in suitable open-necked, white shirts with epaulettes bearing gold braided insignia of rank.

The Captain headed the middle of the three tables which were sited in line across the room. In his company was a mix of his officers and passengers. This arrangement also applied to the forward table headed by the Chief Engineer. The third of the eight-seat tables was set aside for junior officers who, generally, were more punctual and consequently first to leave. Though uniforms were worn, the evening mealtimes were socially informal. Usually the juniors' table issued out a polite exchange of lively banter seemingly in complete oblivion to the Captain's presence. Having the Radio Officer in their midst this group was a principal source of up-to-date information. Between the inevitable bouts of talking shop either one or other officer seated elsewhere would realise it was Saturday evening and sporting events would be concluding for the day. Instinctively they would turn to the far table and, as though switching to BBC 'Grandstand', they could receive full coverage on either cricket scores, race winners or tennis results.

Though Brazendale subscribed to this desultory mode of conversation, one felt that his contribution was not deep rooted. His dialogue came in dutiful packages rather than from a sincere wish to be involved. The increased amount of 'roll' which the passengers accepted with no more than a few high-spirited jokes reminded him the ship was steadily approaching The Skaw. To a lesser acclaim, The Skaw is akin to an inverted Cape Horn. Like that notorious South American landmark the going can get rough there; but Brazendale was not plagued with the thoughts of heavy weather, purely The Skaw, fortuitous to The Horn, marked an important milestone and turning point on the route. Gone nightfall he would be on the bridge with his Third Officer to see the ship safely round.

Skagen is Denmark's most northerly town. It straddles across the tip of the Jutland Peninsula.

Later, in the smoke room, Chief Engineer Clive Buchan and Catering Officer John Garvey recaptured some of the more dramatic moments aboard the ship for the benefit of Bob and Ruth Turnbull. Both men had crewed the *Baltic Enterprise* since her maiden voyage, so much of this armchair sailing was first-hand issue. There were stories of force ten gales with waves that hit the ship like cannon fire; twisted radar aerials and furniture heaped against bulkheads, smashed deck gear and injured seamen. Then there was Baltic ice with the ship ramming, screwing and tearing to free herself with every ounce of power that could be mustered. Icebreakers cutting freeways through one metre thick pressure ice that closed in again within minutes.

"One winter night in the Baltic we met a northerly gale and punched into it all the way to Helsinki. When the deck crew braved to venture to the foredeck at dawn they found that the continuous bludgeoning of big seas had left sea spray that had frozen on every square inch of steel. In places this rime was almost one foot thick; it was estimated that we were coated with four hundred tons of Baltic Sea ice."

Clive Buchan called to the Third Engineer at the bar who produced several colour photographs which clearly showed this. There was no end to these intriguing tales that passed this time of day for the following week.

The conversation at the bar was of cars. Paul Davey revealing intimate details of how he had converted a wrecked Ford 'Pop' into a Formula One hot rod! Philip Rowe's contribution being his exploits as a one-time car transporter driver.

Such was the way in which the evenings started, but all too soon the socialising would diminish into a state of anticlimax. The work style of these mariners did not allow for an indefinite period of relaxation. Again watch-keeping cast a tight net of constraint upon them. Those who were scheduled for the eight to midnight stint were continually aware of the hour hand; drinks were out; there was insufficient time for board games.

When relieved the Chief Officer and Second Engineer would drop in for just one drink, generally pass the time of day and, with thoughts of the 04.00hrs watch would turn in for an early night. The hard part of the bargain did not rest entirely upon these watch-keepers. The Master, who was seldom seen socially in the smoke room, would from time to time appear at the doorway and ask Buchan or Garvey if they could 'spare a minute', this being a polite opening to an hour spent over the inevitable paperwork that a master has to contend with on every voyage. Day workers though they may be, the issues they had to attend to are not fixed to an eight to five day.

On the last haul along the Jutland coastline we took an off-shore glimpse of two seaside towns. Broaching the shore of a sandy promontory was Hirtshals; this small resort with a busy harbour was the Danish terminal for ferries crossing the Skagerrak from Kristiansand and Arendal in southern Norway.

By then the light was giving way to the orange glow of a gathering moon, leaving the view from the ship's starboard rail affording little of descriptive value. Twenty-five miles further on we crept up on Skagan. In daylight we would have seen a thriving resort thronged with summer holidaymakers. However at 11pm this northernmost town of Denmark was represented by a widespread forest of twinkling lights that mirrored in the two miles of dividing ocean.

At The Skaw, 462 miles and 27 hours of sailing lay behind us. We had been advised that after dark this 'lands end' would have nothing of visual interest to offer. But like the Turnbulls I had to see for myself. Here a two mile spit of sandy ground terminates in a narrow point crowned by the 160-foot Grenen Lighthouse. Its powerful beam being the only evidence of our whereabouts.

On and on our mile-hungry ro-ro sailed, with the Grenen light weakening astern. There was much silver-glittered sea but little suggestion of land about us when a call of, "One three zero!" had our ranging bow heading towards waters new. Though The Skaw had not provided the day with the finale that we had hoped for we were not to be dismayed. For out of a miniature constellation of moving ships came a belated treat. This was in the form of a large passenger ferry bedecked with a tiara of glittering lights. As she glided in graceful silence only a half mile distant we watched from the port rail and then ambled aft to see her exit over the stern. We never discovered her name, it did not seem important – our day was complete.

At The Skaw the 160-foot Grenen Lighthouse stands as sentinel over the meeting point of the Skagerrak, Kattegat and North Sea.

5. Onboard Geography

M.V. *Baltic Enterprise* was built as yard no. 209 at Rauma-Repola Oy, Rauma, Finland. On completion in mid-1973 it was said that she was the first ship to be built for British owners by a Finnish yard. Six months later her twin sister, *Baltic Progress*, was placed second on the list. These two ships were the last in line of five identical ro-ros, ultimately labelled as the 'Antares' class, to be launched at Rauma. Apart from the original, *Antares*, which was eventually sold to other European interests, they were purpose-built for the U.K.–Finland, Finanglia Ferries operation. Though the *Baltic Enterprise* had barely strayed off this route, one-off calls had occasionally been made embracing such places as Gothenburg, Helsingborg, Rotterdam, Antwerp and Gydnia. Likewise the *Baltic Progress* and the Finnish-owned *Orion* had made similar diversions.

The main exception to this incessant 'ferrying' was in the case of the second of the Finnish-owned twins, *Sirius*. During April 1976 there was a dock strike that involved all Finnish ports which 'locked in' many ships waiting to off-load there. At the time the *Sirius* was discharging at Hull so her owners, The Finland Steamship Company, decided not to let their ship get tied up in this way and released her on a one-off charter. This took her from Hull, in ballast, to Montreal where she loaded sectional buildings for the Red Sea port of Jeddah. Returning to Hull *Sirius* had notched-up 13,000n.m. in a period of six weeks.

When ships are built in batches they adhere to an area of uniformity that precludes any major individual characteristics. Externally, the obvious distinguishing features between the two Finnish ships and the U.B.C. sisters were the differential in house colours and marks. Structurally, all four ships were identical to the last seam. However, there were some differences where the internal layout of the accommodation area was concerned. In the main this was brought about to provide for the variation in staffing arrangements that existed between British and Finnish crewed ships.

Having Finnish birthright, it was not surprising to find more than a gentle hint of Scandinavia integrated through the living area of the

Baltic Enterprise. Without exception the furnishings, fittings and décor were to the high standard long associated with such ancestry. Nowhere had the comfort of officers, passengers and crewmen been compromised. Without being frilly or fussy the interior incorporated a fair share of the refinements that determine sea-going luxury – functional comforts rather than overbearing sumptuousness. Essentially all the accommodation was encompassed within the five-tier high superstructure.

Monkey Island
Up top, the 'Monkey Island' was no more than the deck-head to the Bridgehouse and adjacent rooms situated on the Navigating Bridge Deck. It was a deck purely in a pedestrian sense – it contained no buildings nor offered any shelter – strictly a place for oceans of fresh air and unimpeded sea views, nothing else.

Navigating Bridge Deck
Apart from the Weather Deck, which was strictly a working area, the Navigating Bridge Deck offered more open deck space than any other. Running aft from the bridge wings were broad deck walkways that provided a marginal level of shelter from the headway winds. Consequently this deck was most favoured by the passengers to spread their deck chairs and sun loungers. Within the Bridgehouse one felt the true width of the ship. Spread across the rear bulkhead of this capacious nerve centre were three internal doors through which could be found a toilet, the main stairway and the Captain's sea cabin respectively. The 'sea cabin' was a small room sparingly furnished with a bed-settee, book shelves, desk and a chair. The Master would use this temporary accommodation during long spells of bad weather when his presence on the bridge is required at all times.

Beyond the central self-closing door a U-shaped landing opened the way to the Radio Room and Radio Officer's quarters to port. As to the equivalent space to starboard there was a door from which a level pitched whine was perpetually emitted. Here I was shown a room which housed the internal telephone exchange plus banks of impressive electronic instruments akin to the radar, gyro compass and other gadgetry upon which an advanced ship of the 1970s relied.

Bridge Deck

Descending a blue, panelled stairway that led from the Bridgehouse one was confronted with a wall display in the form of a large Admiralty chart covering both North and Baltic Seas. Purely for decorative purposes it had been carefully coloured in and boldly marked with the courses the ship plied between Hull and the Finnish ports. The Bridge Deck housed the main living area of the Captain, Chief Engineer and passengers. This was, of course, the most elegant accommodation aboard and it was so arranged to take full advantage of the ship's generous beam. The Captain's quarters, which comprised sleeping, bathroom, lounge and office areas were laid out in an L-shaped fashion at the starboard leading corner of the block. The Chief Engineer was accommodated correspondingly at the port corner and like the Captain enjoyed natural light through forward and side facing windows.

Filling a prodigious amount of space that spread between these suites was a pair of 'king sized', two-berth passenger cabins. To use the word 'spacious' would under-emphasise the volume of these cabins, but to say that each covered a space that would be taken up by four standard ferry ship cabins would not be far from accurate. As sole occupant of the starboard-hand mentioned apartment for the duration of the voyage, I welcomed the space for use as a working base. Linking the widespread walls was a royal blue carpet with which the remainder of the soft furnishings blended. The two side by side oversized single berths, separated by a wooden bedside unit were covered with duvets – a convenience appreciated by the cabin stewards. There was what seemed to be sufficient drawer, cupboard and wardrobe space to swallow the luggage of a royal household and, apart from a cleverly designed dressing table that converted to a writing desk, a table and two lounge chairs were provided. Concealed lighting both within the white-panelled deck-head and behind a full width window pelmet gave soft but adequate illumination. The en suite toilet, lined in hard laminate panels with Scandinavian pine ceiling, was fitted with w.c., washbasin and shower which was fed with an endless supply of piping hot water at all times.

On the debit side the cabin held but one disappointment – the view from the two forward facing windows was badly obstructed. While at sea the Weather Deck gantry crane was parked and locked in position close to the forward end of the superstructure. Its huge crossbeam winged athwart ships in direct line with the Bridge Deck forward cabins. Subsequently one had the option of peering above the beam to acquire a view of the heavens or beneath to see a colourful but uninteresting array of deck freight. For anyone unlike myself who wished to spend the lion's share of the voyage in the cabin this would be an irritating factor. For me the cabin was a place for work and rest. This I did in more than ample comfort.

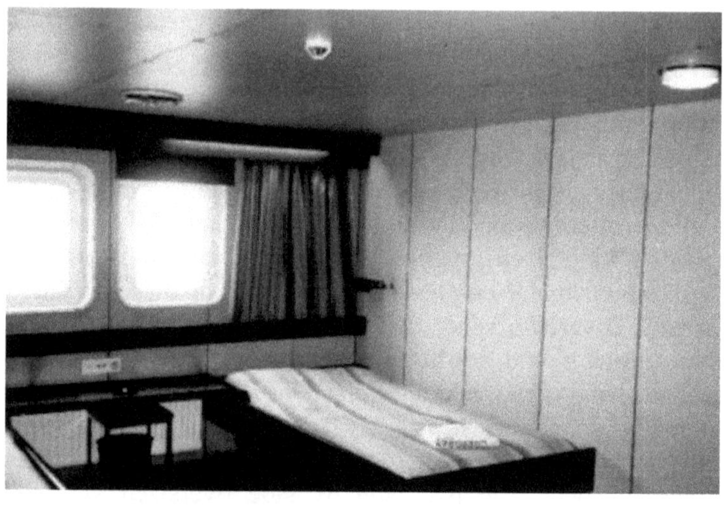

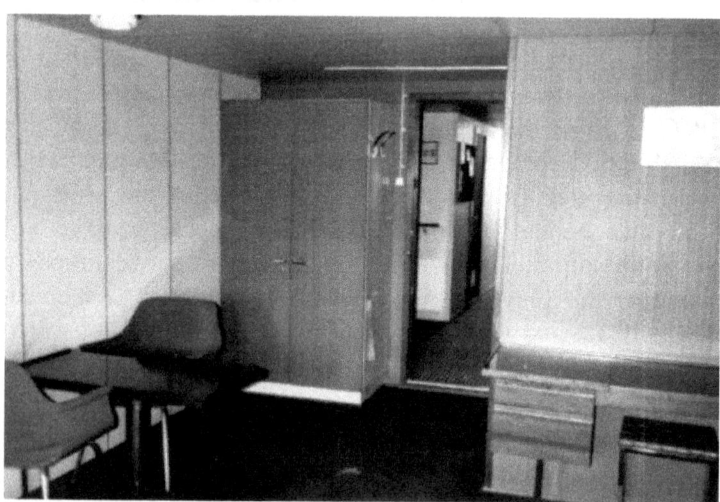

One of the two spacious forward facing passenger cabins.

The four cabins described led out onto a broad alleyway that ran the full width of the accommodation block. Here, fixed centrally on its dark brown bulkhead, was a beautifully etched sheet of glass. Discreetly illuminated this decoration featured a fully rigged Ship of the Line, a 19th century paddle steamer and a profile of the *Baltic Enterprise*, all superimposed against a dark coloured background in the form of a map of Scandinavia. The effect was most pleasing and being prominently displayed won much admiration from the passengers.

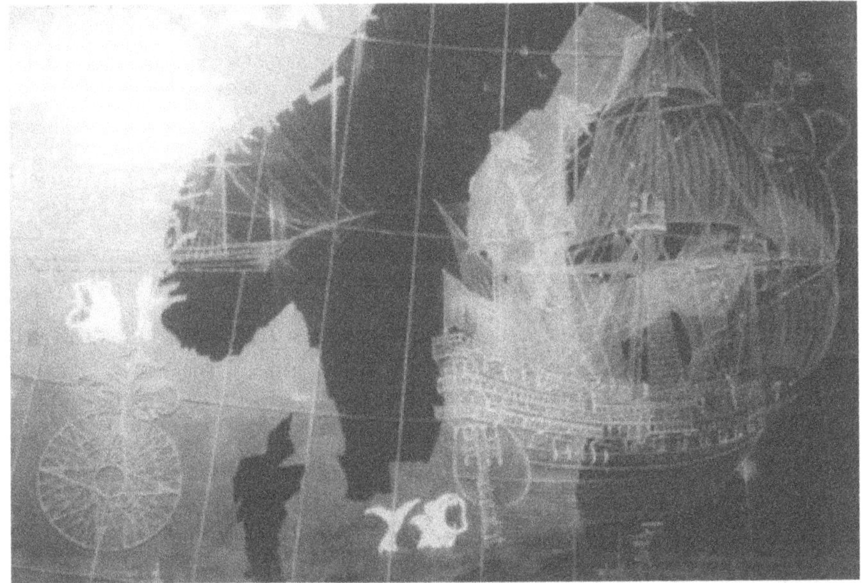

A discreetly illuminated etched glass artwork graced the Bridge Deck stair head.

As in all areas of the Bridge Deck the alleyways were carpeted wall to wall. Two such warmly covered corridors ran aft from the main stairhead concourse. Over to the starboard side this provided four more passenger cabins and a small, infrequently used sitting room. The port side alleyway led to the Dining Saloon, the steward's Serving Pantry and, aftermost, the Lounge where passengers could while away abundant sea-borne hours.

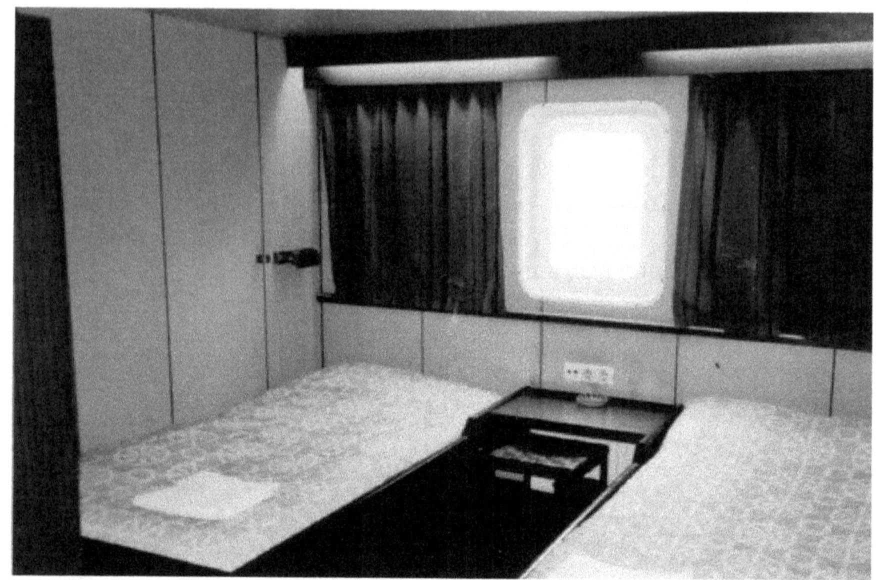

There were four en suite two-berth passenger cabins on the starboard side.

Although only half the size of the forward suites, the four starboard side passenger cabins incorporated the same amenities. Each enjoyed sea views through a single window overlooking the Bridge Deck walkway. The compactness seemed to inspire a cosiness that the larger cabins lacked – a feature probably more appreciated on a long ice-bound winter voyage. The sitting room was distinctly furnished with a large circular mahogany table, six occasional chairs, a wall fixed settee, and an impressive floor to ceiling wall unit that held board games, books and the like.

Measuring thirty feet by sixteen feet the Dining Saloon was far the largest room aboard ship. Here soft furnishings were in blending tones of sage green and mustard, while the main décor was again based on sapele woodgrain panels together with the restful oatmeal colour of hessian wall covering. Overlooking the port side and feeding natural light into the saloon were six rectangular windows – two at the end of each across-ships table. Directly opposite, and dominating the long inner wall, was a fifty-six square foot mural depicting the maritime history of Hull. With ambitious use of colour, its creator Keith Hemsby had formulated a kaleidoscope of ships, landmarks and prominent figures covering the heydays of the port; much the largest inset being a side profile of the *Baltic Enterprise* which ran the full length of the mural base.

The port side Dining Saloon was furnished with three eight-seat tables.

Tables were permanently covered in snow-white linen, and typewritten menu cards were placed on each at mealtimes. For all that the menus were based on traditional British fare the choice of dishes remained surprisingly varied throughout the duration of the voyage. These menus stood the same in both the Bridge Deck Dining Saloon and the seamen's Main Deck mess room. Regardless of captain, passenger or pantry boy everyone aboard had the same choice of food.

For passengers morning coffee and afternoon tea broke the interval between the meals, this was served in their own dedicated lounge situated directly aft of the dining saloon pantry. At the given time the duty steward would quietly serve the small group. As the biscuits were passed around tea, coffee and hot water would flow copiously from the silver plate pots.

Though pleasantly furnished with a three-piece lounge suite, several occasional chairs and a mahogany sideboard unit, the passenger lounge never induced an air of cosiness.

Primarily this was due to an external doorway that provided direct access to the outer deck. During the run of good weather the lounge could become something of a passageway, for throughout the daytime the door was almost continually open. On indifferent days those seeking a breath of sea air would unavoidably allow a blast of cold air to circle the room as they hurried to close the portal.

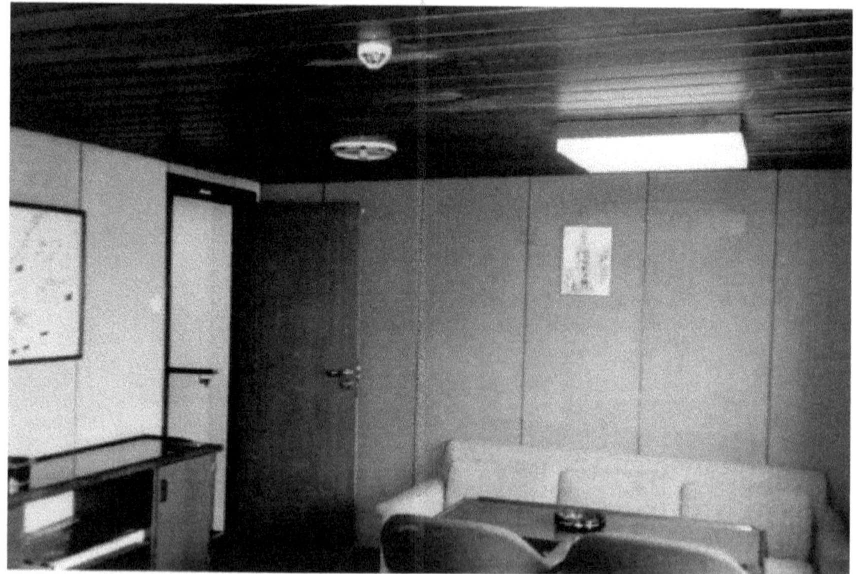

The Passenger Lounge was one of two comfortable Bridge Deck sanctuaries.

Boat Deck

A wall mounted clock, conveniently sited in the stairway between the Bridge and Boat Decks, was always fixed on B.S.T.; in effect this halved the two hour differential between Greenwich Mean and Finnish time. While in Finland the ship's clocks read one hour late – at U.K. ports in wintertime they were one hour early.

When on the Boat Deck one could be said to be in the heart of the ship's accommodation. Here eight officers were housed – five in forward cabins overlooking the Weather Deck and three down the starboard side. The alleyways ran in unison with those on the Bridge Deck above, but their décor came in more striking contrasts – two-tone blue for the walls or bulkheads, while the deck head was in bright orange. Carpet runners stretched the full fifty-foot length of the fore-aft passages, which were permanently lit by flush overhead fitments.

Space allocated for the individual apartments was related to seniority of rank or the role they had to fulfil. Nevertheless each officer had more than sufficient space in smart surroundings. All the Boat Deck cabins had their own private facilities including a sitting area that contained refinements such as a drinks refrigerator and concealed lighting. In common with many ship owners U.B.C. allowed wives of officers to accompany them on a limited number of voyages each year. Consequently the sleeping section in the Boat Deck cabins contained a double bed.

The Ship's Office and Liquor Bond Store were located at opposite ends of the starboard alleyway. Unattended behind closed doors the Ship's Office was more of a registry than a place of commercial activity. Filing cabinets containing an accumulation of ship's records made up the bulk of the office furniture, however one thing noted was a Telecom 'pay phone'. On docking in the U.K. this was quickly linked to the normal Telecom grid, allowing crew to dial home direct from the ship.

Away from port the Bond locker was a much busier enterprise. Here, while the ship was at sea, beers, wines, spirits and cigarettes were sold under the strict control of the Catering Officer at off-duty prices. I was told that the sale of spirits was restricted to officers and passengers. The seamen's tipple was restricted to beer or lager excepting when 'paying off' the ship. They were then allowed to purchase the normal duty-free quota.

The Officers' Smoke Room bar was a product of crew members' DIY skills.

Originally the officers' Smoke Room was 'dry.' The copper-topped bar came through the ingenuity of several members of the crew; effectively set across one corner of the room it helped to conjure up the atmosphere one expected to find in the local pub. Before this addition, drinking (such as it was on short-sea voyages) was restricted to individuals having to buy a supply for consumption in their cabins. Now the port side Smoke Room was their social centre and although it was originally intended for their own use they normally opened a warm invitation to all passengers. Bar duties were carried out by the officers themselves on a roster that worked in with the normal watch-keeping system. Compared to shore prices, bar costs at the 'Enterprise Bar' were ridiculously low. Even so small profits were made, sufficient to provide extra items for the room – records, tapes, books and games. The remainder was donated to charitable organisations; the R.N.L.I. and children's homes being mentioned.

A few paces further aft along the port side alleyway was the officers' Mess Room. As aforementioned this fitted as an alternative eating place for those who were unable to forfeit sufficient time to change for the dressier Bridge Deck Dining Saloon. This was definitely a place of their own, somewhere to let off steam, a private den where blunt and earthy banter could flow across the tables without caution. Adorning the cream, panelled walls and adding to the air of masculinity was a well used dartboard and, naturally, the usual 'girlie' calendar.

Next door, a complete contrast. Coming from Finnish stock *Enterprise* had inherited part and parcel of the national constitution – the sauna. Having the natural pine cabin hot room built within a complex that included three shower cubicles, wash basins, toilet, changing and rest areas, it compared with any well equipped shore sauna. Normally the officers used this amenity in small groups during the evening or night depending on watch commitments. Passengers were free to use the sauna during the daytime; a reservation board was provided for those wishing to 'indulge'.

Completing the Boat Deck accommodation was a small laundry. This windowless area, situated aft of the sauna, was equipped with two twin-tub washing machines and an ever-hot drying room. This facility was there to enable each officer to keep up to date with small items of washing that accumulate after a week or so at sea. The main bulk of the ship's laundry, bed and table linen, was collected by contractors each time she arrived at Hull.

Officers on each U.B.C. ro-ro ship took leave on a 50-50 basis. Usually this meant that each man completed three round voyages then took leave for the equivalent amount of time. Consequently the ship had a complement of officers to form two complete crews. These crews did not change over en bloc. Therefore on completion of a voyage there were always one or two men leaving the ship and newcomers arriving to step into their shoes. The seamen's leave was less generous – they worked a two-voyage on, one-voyage off basis, each man spending eight months of the year aboard to the officers' six.

Main Deck

The fifteen seamen aboard the *Baltic Enterprise* were housed on the Main Deck. This represented the 'ground floor' of the accommodation block. Each man had his own separate cabin, though less spacious and palatial than the aforementioned it was smartly furnished with a single berth, wash basin, storage units, table and chair. The Bo'sun and Senior

Cook had the additional amenity of an en suite shower and toilet. From the port side alleyway they had access to a combined dining and recreation room, a laundry and a fully equipped sauna complex. Again, colour schemes were based towards contrasting combinations of blue, orange and oatmeal with widespread use of hard laminate surfaces; as throughout the ship, sapele woodgrain internal doors being the norm.

Living space on the Main Deck was less abundant than elsewhere. Internally the clinically clean galley with its attendant dry and refrigerated stores absorbed a substantial portion of the after end. Outdoors, at that level, a broad through-way, allowing vehicular access between weather and after decks down the starboard side, took a considerable slice off the block.

Several monochrome television sets were dotted around the accommodation. Though intended to receive a wide range of continental channels, reception was greatly limited and inconsistent. On leaving U.K. shores the picture very soon diminished beyond legibility. In Baltic waters Swedish television programmes sometimes came loud and clear, but often such viewing was spoiled as the ship moved further away from the transmitter. I was not unduly perturbed; neither were the rest of the passengers, after all we hadn't gone to sea to watch T.V.

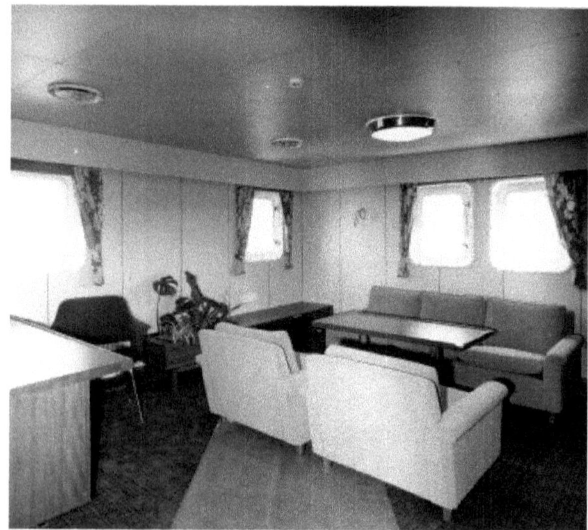

The captain's three-roomed cabin area was located on the starboard side of the Bridge Deck. The Chief Engineer was similarly accommodated on the port side.

6. Scandinavian Shores

At more than one hundred sea miles south of The Skaw the Kattegat's expansive waters narrow abruptly until its outlying shores merge to within two miles. From the east, Sweden fronts onto the channel in an endless green ribbon of shore-struck conifer forests. Hereabouts, on the western flank, Denmark's contribution is little different – just occasional clusters of beach bungalows leisurely spread affront of the pines offering relief to an otherwise featureless onshore panorama. The land here is Zealand, the largest and most populated of Denmark's numerous islands.

At 05.30hrs, in brilliant sunshine, *Baltic Enterprise* thrust her 460-foot long bulk centrally along the narrowing wedge of water. Throughout the early hours of Sunday we had poured down the Kattegat leaving Gothenburg, Varberg and Falkenberg to port while the tiny islands of Laeso and Anholt were likewise discarded unseen beyond our starboard quarter. Around the 04.00hrs watch changeover we had been put on a heading of 162 degrees and it was that course that carried us towards the funnel neck of The Sound. We were now well and truly in Scandinavian waters and would remain so for much of the next six days.

Captain Gerry Brazendale had risen early to join his Chief Officer on the bridge. Both, lightly dressed in shirt sleeves and sporting dark glasses against low but powerfully reflective sunlight, paced intermittently between the bridge facia, chart table and the port wing. Certainly the hour did not help to promote a flood of conversation between the two navigators. It had gone without saying that the Master's presence was due to the fact that we were rapidly approaching a forty mile stretch of busy and often congested waterway. His business was to pilot his ship through these testing reaches until such time as the fairway opened up to the Baltic Sea. Though Peter Green had guided *Enterprise* accurately to the mouth of The Sound he had automatically assumed the role of Brazendale's aide.

"I think we will have a man on the wheel now Peter."

Having made an extensive probe of the silver-blue waterway beyond the ship's head Brazendale had finally broken a long silence. Green quietly moved over to the internal phone and dialled the crew's quarters.

"One six five please," was the call as the seaman settled behind the wheel three minutes later.

"Steady one six five sir."

In anticipation Green was at the autopilot control effecting the changeover to manual steering. Nine miles further on and thirty minutes later, still holding the eighteen and a half knots we had adopted on leaving the Humber, *Enterprise's* exhausts ricocheted over a shimmering waterway flanked by the buildings of two towns. It is here that Helsingborg in Sweden and Helsingor on the Danish shore face each other across the narrowest reach of The Sound. Throughout the day small car ferries ply continuously between the two centres. In addition countless summertime pleasure craft take advantage of these sheltered waters. Consequently vigilance is the operative word for those on the bridge of large commercial vessels making a through passage.

Following my almost nocturnal observations through the angled screens of the bridgehouse I had made for the open air of the monkey island. From there, apart from a number of early morning sailors weaving dinghies close to the shore, the view was one of an unimpeded road of flat silver sea reaching between the two countries until it merged with an empty sky many miles ahead.

The most striking feature on approaching Helsingor was the sighting of Kronborg Castle. The castle, which is world famous through being the setting of Shakespeare's 'Hamlet' was sited on a small promontory that allowed the waters of The Sound to lap within feet of its base. Beyond the sunlit ramparts and green copper pinnacles of Kronborg, Helsingor was set on rising land pleasantly decked with broad leafed trees. The town flourished during the 13th century when the sea route round The Skaw came into common use. At that time 'Sound' dues were imposed and a bronze cannon, which was now on display beneath the castle walls, was used to enforce this levy. Unfortunately I was unable to see it from our hurrying ro-ro – but luckily we did not hear it!

Through the nautical rule-of-the-road our course favoured the Danish shore leaving the opposite bank best viewed through binoculars. Here sleeping Helsingborg stood embellished with aurora of morning light. Within its precincts Helsingborg displays vast contrasts of architecture, notably medieval towers, 18th century palaces and mansions together with ultra modern buildings.

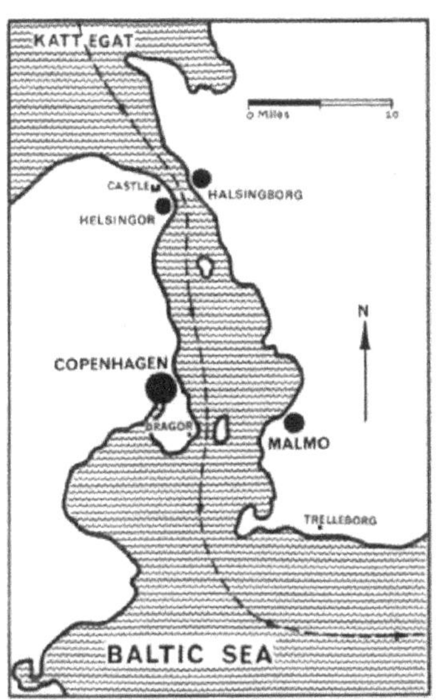

Linking the Kattegat and Baltic Sea, the waters of The Sound break onto the shores of Denmark to the west and Sweden to the east, The *Baltic Enterprise* held her service speed of 18.5 knots for the greater part of the sixty mile passage. (FotoFlite.)

Kronborg (Hamlet's) Castle was clearly seen on the passage southwards through 'The Sound'.

Being a thriving port the dock area was, of course, a prominent feature on the waterfront. Neatly spaced along the harbour walls were dozens of white flagpoles. I was told that when a ship enters Helsingborg a flag, representative of her country of origin, is hoisted. On that occasion the flag poles were bare; clearly all the flags were taken down at night and not hoisted again until some sensible hour!

Soon the twin towns were falling astern. While I pondered at the rail over their withdrawal, ferry boats pulled out to cross The Sound from either shore. The time was 06.10hrs and I guessed that these were the first ferries of the day. Danes and Swedes continually cross to each other's territory and here the Helsingborg-bound ferry wasted no time in crossing astern of us, quickly dissecting the road of foaming wake that we had embossed along the channel.

Having by then sailed 590n.m. and 35 hours out of Hull, we were just past the halfway stage to Helsinki. From time to time I would hear Brazendale call course changes to the helmsman – 178 – 180 – 183; being bound for one of the world's northernmost capitals this leg carrying us due south was somewhat surreal. Luckily, as the two shorelines progressively opened up, the buoyed channel that we followed continued to carry us within viewing distance of the Danish seaboard. Often we passed close by islands and islets. Some had small holiday cabins perched among groves of fresh green conifers; others were no more than rocky outcrops poking through the surface. One island alone fell into a category totally uncharacteristic of that peaceful Sunday morning scene – here, as a sign of the times, lay an island of modern defence systems. Rising from the rocky terrain of this waterborne stronghold named Middelgrund were plinths of concrete bearing fearsome ballistic missiles that pointed in each and every direction. Not a place to dwell upon; in fact somewhere left well astern – which it soon was.

By 07.15, still hauling southwards, we were abeam of Copenhagen. Rising from land barely a few feet above sea level, Denmark's capital, viewed from the sea, gave the impression of a northern Venice. Though more than a mile away the Copenhagen skyline was as clear as it was varied. The vista showed an array of modern commercial high-rise buildings amid the coppered roofs and golden spires of architectural masterpieces. From being a small village in the 11th century, Copenhagen steadily grew in size and importance, and in the 15th century the King went to live there. With the accession of King Christian IV (1588-1648) the then prosperous city entered into a great period of expansion. Christian was a man of extraordinary energy and possessed a passion for building. He was responsible for many of the Renaissance-style buildings that we could pick out from the decks of our ship. Copenhagen being the home of more than a million Danes, which represents one quarter of the country's population, is the largest of the Scandinavian capitals.

All too soon the six miles of quays and installations that faced the main waterway were falling behind our starboard quarter. However our sustained contact with the shoreline brought reward through our approach to the main runway of Copenhagen's international airport at Kastrup. The eastern extremity of the broad tarmac with its battery of approach lights pushes out towards the water until the tideway almost licks at the undercarriages of landing aircraft. What seemed to be one of the timeliest incidents of the voyage was the arrival of a Boeing 747 nigh to the time *Enterprise* levelled across the end of the runway. It briefly cast an enormous shadow over the ship. Simultaneously the roar of its jets temporarily muted the relentless bark offered from our funnel top.

The airport is situated on Amager, a pear-shaped island that is linked to Copenhagen by its harbour bridges. Together with Malmö Airport, ten miles across The Sound, Kastrup had reached its operational limit. In solution (at the time of writing) it had been proposed to develop a new joint international airport on the mid-Sound island of Saltholm. The plan includes a four mile tunnel to Denmark while a six mile bridge would link the island to Sweden.

No sooner had the noise of the aircraft landing subsided when there was a distinct change in the attitude of the ship. The concurrent sounds and pulsations created through muscling at full service speed had become an integral part of the ship's make-up, insomuch as one's senses become dulled or even, to some degree, oblivious to their existence. Only when this chain is broken or changed does one become fully awake to its monotony.

We had arrived at the Drogden channel where, on what was visually an expanse of water, the marks and buoys had appreciatively narrowed the navigational fairway. Brazendale had cut our headway down to eight knots for not only was there less elbow room but we were suddenly among other traffic. Ahead, and approaching, was a freighter of considerable tonnage that was following in the wake of a deeply laden coaster. Astern was a large car ferry which, like us, was making for the

Baltic, while creeping down our port side was a pair of small tug boats. They were coping with a huge box-square barge piled as high as a house with what appeared enough timber to build a 'Noah's Ark.'

"One hell of a pile of matchsticks," was Brazendale's comment after offering a cursory wave to the tug men.

Ten miles beyond Drogden the Sound gave way to the southern reaches of the Baltic Sea. Here the ship re-established her mood of urgency arrowing her white, roller bow wave south-eastwards into the warmth of the midsummer morning. Whereas at the dawn of the day the decks had been devoid of human activity, now they were subjected to the steady comings and goings of both crew and passengers. After the breakfast tables had been cleared the stewards busied themselves with Hoovers, furniture polish and dusters. They pounded the alleyway carpets, leathered the internal window surfaces and moved from cabin to cabin adding further lustre to seemingly immaculate furniture and fittings. Though this was part and parcel of their everyday routine, Sunday was of special importance.

Traditionally, throughout the merchant service Sunday morning is the occasion of the Captain's weekly inspection. I don't suppose the procedure on U.B.C. ships differed greatly to that on any other line. Here, accompanied by his Chief and Catering Officers, the Captain starts at the topmost deck and inspects the entire accommodation area. Checking each and every cabin, mess room, lounge, broom cupboard, alleyway and fire-point, the Master makes comment to his subordinates who list for correction the items that have met with his disapproval.

Rounding Sweden's southernmost limit, our course became more easterly allowing the sun to pour down the starboard side. Consequently out came the deck chairs and out came my travelling companions. The sea state was flat calm – no waves, just a progression of silver-crested ripples. While musing at the distant coastline over to port I was joined by Second Engineer John Gunning. Commenting on my remarks about the excellent weather conditions over the past two days John Gunning sensed that a change was imminent. Whether he had heard a local forecast or was relying on instinct I do not know. Later, what I did discover was that the Second Engineer was something of an authority on Baltic weather.

John Gunning, mid-thirties and single, was a soft spoken East Anglian. Though he had joined U.B.C. two years previously and crewed the *Baltic Enterprise* for barely eighteen months one could sense his genuine affinity with the ship. Not that he had singled out *Enterprise* as a special ship in his life; I felt that his references of 'old girl' could have been applied to any ship on which he had served. Gunning wasn't aboard purely as a means to making a living; he was there because he liked the life. At that time he had recently taken time off to sit for his Chief Engineer's certificate – I later was told that he had been successful.

The off-watch Second Engineer and I ambled along the green deck until we arrived at the open bridgehouse door. Here, with the ship now in more open water, at her service speed, and steering on automatic pilot, we found Third Officer Willie Maclaughlan alone on watch.

"All alone I see young Willie." John Gunning's Norfolk accent broke the bridgehouse quiet and brought the Scotsman away from a radar console.

"Ay, I reckon the old man will be on his inspection by now." Maclaughlan greeted his fellow officer with spontaneous shipboard cross-talk.

"George is out there though." He indicated through the forward windows at Electrical Engineer George Hall perched on the high platform of the weather deck gantry crane apparently working on a faulty circuit. "I don't know if I am supposed to keep an eye on him or if he is there to spy on me!"

"What is our ETA at Helsinki?" my companion enquired.

"At this pace it will be tomorrow, mid-afternoon."

The young Third Officer led us over to the chart table where he busied himself with dividers.

"I make it 14.00 at Harmaja Pilot Station so that should be 15.00 on the berth our time."

Willie Maclaughlan showed me the course we were taking across the chart. We were about to start a haul of two hundred and fifty miles on a heading of 060. This heading would shortly carry us past the Danish island of Bornholm and ultimately to the mid-Baltic, east of the largest of its islands – Gotland. At that time we were almost seven hundred nautical miles and forty hours sailing out of Hull.

The face of Bornholm's northern cliffs showed up through the glasses right on the call for Sunday lunch. However I held on for a few minutes to gain a four mile, onshore impression of the island. Being a popular holiday venue for thousands of Scandinavians, Bornholm is one of Denmark's great assets. Known as 'The Pearl of the Baltic' its gently rolling countryside is scattered with tiny farmsteads and round churches. Denmark possesses little mineral wealth, but Bornholm has massive granite deposits. The solid grey rock of the northern part of its seventy mile shoreline bore evidence to this claim.

While in the southern Baltic Sea the Danish island of Bornholm was sighted four miles distant on our starboard side.

When the situation allowed for it, siestas were a small luxury *Enterprise*'s officers took advantage of. That is to say should the ship be at sea in fair weather the men who were off duty would manage to squeeze a couple of hours of early afternoon relaxation. Up to the time afternoon tea was served, the Dining Saloon would empty and cabin doors would close on hushed alleyways; there was a kind of reverence about that period of the day which passengers respected. If out and about during this time of day one would surreptitiously tread the alleyways more lightly, voices would be toned down and doors would be closed with a greater degree of care. It was not the ideal opportunity for seeking the Catering Officer to purchase cigarettes, chocolates or sprits. Nor was it time to be looking for the Captain or Chief Officer to ask questions of no immediate importance.

With Sunday lunch completed, people moving to quiet corners of the accommodation or decks and with Bornholm Island fading into a hazy image on the distant horizon, I duly retired to catch up with my notes. Within the hour, as I sat at a desk filled with papers, tape recordings, chart sections and the like, there was a cautious knock at my cabin door.

Bob Turnbull had been keeping Bernard Elworthy company during his 12.00-16.00 bridge watch. The Second Officer believed we would soon be within sight of the largest and fastest ferry ship afloat. Bob, as enthusiastic as I, could not wait to pass on the information. On noticing a rapidly advancing 'blip'' on our long range radar, Bernard had kept more than the normal routine interest. The response was eating its way across the range rings at nearly twice the normal expected pace; his instinct had told him that it could only be one ship – the 23,000gt *Finnjet*.

During her early years in service the *Finnjet* powered across the Baltic at speeds in excess of thirty knots.

The three of us stood on the bridge wing as, on a reciprocal bearing, but in a gathering haze, *Finnjet* stormed rapidly towards us several points over to port. As the closing speed between *Enterprise* and this 37,500 horsepower, gas turbine propelled passenger ferry was somewhere in the order of 50 knots, it was not long before, with a one mile gap abeam, the two ships were passing.

During the early 1970s, Oy Finnlines of Helsinki, evaluated the long term of Baltic passenger traffic. Following much detailed project work the idea of using one super ferry instead of three normal vessels evolved. Subsequently an order was placed and, in 1977, the *Finnjet* entered service on the Helsinki-Travemünde, West Germany route. Operating at over thirty knots this 1,600-passenger berth superferry was capable of completing the 1,300-mile round voyage in two days.

Seeing the *Finnjet* tearing through the Baltic that day had been an unexpected bonus, moreover, soon afterwards there had been a marked deterioration in visibility. After our contact with Bornholm Island we had sailed into a murky sea-level haze yet still overlooked by an immaculate sky of blue. But now the curtain had grown thicker and higher, blotting out the sun and leaving us pounding north-eastwards trammelled within a two-mile radius world of drab sea mist. Now the Baltic was a less attractive place to be in. Its sparkling silver-blue hue had transformed into a ponderous grey wash

.

Being an 'inland' sea the Baltic is sometimes called the 'Mediterranean of the north'. Like this denizen of the south, many races and cultures meet around its shores. In the Middle Ages the Hanseatic League was an alliance of trading towns fronting the Baltic. This was governed from the German town of Lübeck. Though large industrial centres have grown and flourished there since those times, so did political frontiers. Indeed the very trade upon which the United Baltic Corporation was founded was, at the time of this voyage, secured behind the Iron Curtain.

The U.B.C. house flag was first shown around the Baltic in the summer of 1919. It was in the 'between wars' period that the Corporation grew and flourished by providing direct links between the Baltic States and London with a fleet of progressively adaptable and capacious freight ships ultimately carrying up to two hundred passengers. In these early days Danzig (now Gdansk) in Poland and ports in the east Baltic states of Latvia, Lithuania and Estonia were serviced. All ships used the Kiel Canal and branch offices and agencies were opened on the regular routes.

Baltic sailings were suspended throughout the Second World War and the fleet, under Admiralty and Ministry of War direction, saw service in all parts of the world. Four U.B.C. ships were lost through mines or torpedoes. As soon as normal trading conditions returned, Polish services were opened from both London and Hull but other Baltic state services could not be resumed. At this point the U.K–Finland services were inaugurated; the Hull–Leningrad route was added in 1959.

During 1973, to maintain pace with a new generation of shipping expectations the company had introduced the first ro-ro freight ferry to its services – the *Baltic Enterprise*. That August afternoon, sailing to schedule northwards through the Baltic with the U.B.C. house flag proudly tugging at her mainmast, one sensed that the *Baltic Enterprise* was competently manifesting the esteem and stature the company had generated through the challenging decades gone by.

The 1,671gt. *Baltic Jet* was typical of the nine conventional freighters built by the United Baltic Corporation during the 1950s.

7. Engine Room Cacophony– Bridge Composure

Gone Monday noontime we were still pushing north-east on a heading of 060 degrees but now crossing the eastern arm of the Baltic Sea known as the Gulf of Finland. With more than one thousand sea miles behind us we were within three hours of the Helsinki waterfront.

Unfortunately John Gunning's prediction twenty-four hours earlier had been more than accurate. The almost perfect weather conditions that we had enjoyed for the lion's share of the voyage from Hull had disappeared behind an oppressive blanket of sea fog. As if the total loss of visibility were not enough the elements had decided to treat us to frequent heavy showers that lashed at the ship's forward facing windows and puddled her decks throughout the morning.

The sea, grey, dull and uneasy, prompted *Baltic Enterprise* into a motion that could not be characterised as either pitching or rolling. Time and again she would begin to dip her bow towards the troughs of oncoming seas only to change her attitude. This abandonment would lead into a short sequence of lateral restlessness that sometimes was enough to affect the facial reactions of unsteady passengers but seemingly went unnoticed among crew members. Up forward, adding to the precipitation, sea spray was regularly thrust skywards up and over the weather deck cargo. These saturating bouts were continually induced through conflicting efforts of ruffled seas upon the ship's undaunted forward progress.

We had moved from one weather front to another, consequently Gerry Brazendale had been on his bridge ever since the fog had closed in. This uncompassionate turn of events, though intimidating from Sunday lunchtime, had arrived some two hundred miles back. Brazendale's vigil was now in its thirteenth hour. Fog or no fog, not once had our speed been reduced; guided entirely by her navigational systems *Enterprise* had surged through the Baltic at 'ten ahead' holding her schedule almost to the minute. It was not a cold day, yet in protest to the dank realism outdoors high-necked, navy blue pullovers were the uniform chosen for the occasion. Contrasting with the youthful stature of the Second Officer, Brazendale's new garb, opulently showing four gold bar braids at each shoulder, disclosed his portly advancement into middle age. Through hours of peering down at the orange glowing radar consoles his eyes had begun to show the signs of tiredness. So too, on up-righting himself away from the screens, had the habitual removal of flopping hair away from his broad forehead. His drooping fringe was a form of styling that had begun to add further stress to the situation.

This was by no means the first time that Brazendale had guided a ship towards the outlying islands of Finland through adverse weather; neither would it be his last. Nevertheless it was not an assignment a master would savour. Unrelenting he had paced between the main fascia and the chart table checking and counter-checking the information fed by the radar and the Decca Navigator. Infrequently, while on these seemingly automatic excursions across the bridgehouse carpet, he would bisect the path of his watch-keeping officer. The encounter would induce a brief flurry of conversation that never deviated from the job in hand. All three deck officers had stood watch through his long vigil. Each respected his wish to sidestep any other subject. Other than sounds from the ship's instrumentation the only respite from the long spells of silence was that offered every two minutes by the fog siren way out on the mist encircled foremast.

Barely thirty-five miles separated us from the Harmaja Pilot Station. From this island base the pilot would effect a rendezvous and accompany us along the remaining three miles of tightly buoyed water to Helsinki. Racing towards that point, obscured from the outside world, I sensed that the last flicker of relaxation had been extinguished. Making my presence in the bridgehouse as diminutive as possible, I found a remote corner and whiled through my notes of that morning.

From breakfast onwards the accommodation block had seen more activity than at any time over the past three days. With our impending landfall involving the departure of the Jackson family and a more than refreshed transport driver, suitcases were being seen outside cabin doors. Road maps were being spread out on the lounge tables, accounts were being settled and 'duty frees' collected at the catering office.

Irrespective of the inclement weather, my morning had been utilised to full advantage. Following an invitation to see the mechanical side of the ship, 09.30 had seen me collecting ear defenders in the office of Chief Engineer Clive Buchan; with more than twenty-five years service with U.B.C. he was one of the company's more senior engineers.

Tyneside has an age-long tradition of producing first class marine engineers – Clive Buchan was born and bred there – his soft Geordie accent clearly backing this claim. I have always had a good rapport with Tynesiders; this association being no exception.

The sound proofed Engine Control Room.

A section of the engine room.

Our journey to the engine room commenced at a door hinged from the port side alleyway on the Boat Deck. Wearing a grease-stained white boiler suit the Chief led the way onto the first of seven flights of stairs that progressively criss-crossed down a brilliantly lit shaft. At first we seemed to be encompassed within a strong up-draught of hot air. However having dropped three levels the main impact came from hardworking machinery. Regardless of the ear defenders the almighty commotion emitted from below became implanted in each nerve and muscle, gripping every breath of air. Buchan had made the descent a thousand times. For him the dramatic and sudden change from the comparable hush of the living area to this erupting cauldron of noise was of no more consequence than switching on the radio.

Mine was a descent filled with intrigue and caution to the extent that the Chief was looking quizzically upwards when I arrived at the last landing. Putting noise aside the next captivating element was the generous amount of light afforded. Together with the many ranks of strip lights, liberal use of white, cream and light blue gloss paint gave the engine room an almost clinical effect. Down at base level, one felt to be centred in a floodlit arena packed to capacity with all manner of pulsating machinery.

Conversation had been out of the question but following my companion's sign language I was quickly guided inside a sound proofed haven. Seated there, at a bank of multi-dialled consoles was Scotsman Bob Cairns. Together with Paul Davey, Cairns carried the rank of Third Engineer. As we were not carrying a 'Fourth' Cairns had stepped into that watch stint. With all its futuristic animation, sound protection and air conditioning, the control room was a place of sanctuary. There the engineers settle after an initial on-watch half-hour tour of routine checks and adjustments.

The Chief explained his watch-keeper's responsibilities through monitoring the data displayed: "It is vital that any trouble should be spotted and remedial action taken straight away."

Some of the control room instrumentation was a duplicate of that seen on the bridge. Mainly this included dials and gauges giving performance readings of the main engines. Relevant levers offered an alternative engine control position should the bridge system fail. Apart from the obvious importance of propulsion units and generators, a ship relies on a host of auxiliary systems to keep it functional. An assembly of lights that gave warnings of faults within such areas was a prominent feature of the main facia.

With talk of ventilators, compressed air starters, fuel heaters and water supply pressurisation we were only scratching the surface. From then on I realised that to explain the ship's mechanical make-up would require more pages than available in this book and, moreover, someone more qualified than myself to describe them.

Leaving Bob Cairns to his coloured lights, advancing digits, twitching dials and data-filled log books, the Chief led me back-stage. Within this unmanned anti-room were sited three substantial diesel-powered generators that had the output capable of lighting several streets of houses.

"Electricity is the very lifeblood of the ship. Without it almost every single mechanical function – from windlasses to windscreen wipers, radar to refrigerators, and direction finder to domestic services – would grind to an eerie silence." Clive Buchan indicated that only one of the diesels was running. "When we dock, later in the day, all three generators will be called for. It's the cranes, lifts and deck gear that make the meter race round!"

Facing the line-up of generators was a bank of shining grey consoles. They housed a complex of intricate switchgear that was linked to the miles of wiring threaded around the ship.

In the days of sail a ship's engineers were the carpenter and the sail maker. Through their individual skills and versatility in the art of improvisation, ships that were theoretically doomed often limped to safety. Erecting makeshift masts, repairing smashed steering gear and resurrecting shredded sails with ten thousand stitches was their line of business.

Timber and canvas are not commodities easily found on a 1970s ro-ro ship. Consequently the engineers' workshop is equipped to fashion steel. Lathes, drills, grinders and vices were the principal furnishings in this section of *Enterprise*'s engine room complex. Though the ship carried a comprehensive store of mechanical parts, the engineers had to be resourceful. Spread around steel-topped work benches was a variety of oil-clad components. They had been replaced as worn out, faulty or just in need of servicing.

"Costly parts can't be written off at random. If we can repair them on the spot we do so – otherwise they are sent to marine workshops ashore. The majority of the work carried out in this workshop is routine servicing, which is a continuous process." Buchan added: "So you can see there is more to this job than sitting in the control room. These ships are driven hard to maintain schedules unthinkable a decade ago. There is no time in port worthy of mention to carry out general repairs. Only a major breakdown distorts the schedule, even then contingency plans are put into operation. We have put to sea on one engine with engineers working on the defective one. Naturally the weather and tides hold the key to the progress we make under half power; in favourable conditions we have maintained twelve knots or more."

Baltic Enterprise's propulsion units were two Stork-Werkspoor 9TM410 diesels each developing 5,250 b.h.p. at 530 r.p.m. To anyone other than those directly connected with marine engineering this information means little. However if I were to mention that each of these engines weighed eighty-five metric tons, measured twenty-five feet in length and stood some eleven feet in height, the layman should begin to appreciate their size. As a comparison they would simply dwarf a juggernaut lorry engine into looking as though it belonged to a matchbox toy!

From the workshop I followed Clive Buchan onto a catwalk that ran the full length of the starboard engine. Diesel engines consume oxygen in limitless quantities. Sited well below the waterline those of a ship can only be fed from above. Four powerful ventilators were blending a strong down-current of Baltic sea-tinged air with hot, oil-tainted ozone. Amid this swirling mistral we paused. Both these nine-in-line main engines were turning over at 510 r.p.m. – medium speed diesels in marine terms. Through gearing they were revolving fifteen-inch diameter propeller shafts at 200 r.p.m.

Standing at the rail with the nine cylinder heads at knee height, the noise was beyond description. With ear defenders the impression was of the roar at the base of a mighty waterfall. Without them – momentarily I eased the protectors away from my head – the convulsed air reverberated within the grip of a dynamic scream that bludgeoned the ear drums beyond the limit of my expectations. Running as they were in unison, these rasping monsters consumed thirty tons of fuel oil every twenty-four hours; I was assured that this was no greater than expected of a ship with an output in excess of ten thousand horsepower.

On returning aloft to the sanity of the officers' mess, Clive Buchan poured out the mid-morning coffee. At this time of day off-watch officers drifted through the portal of their boat deck retreat. The occasion was known aboard as 'Smoko' – a fifteen minute break where, amid the airing of views over topical issues, tea and coffee of their own brewing flowed from seemingly bottomless pots. Among the now familiar faces of Messrs Green, Hall, Elworthy, Garvey, Davey and Gunning, I began to collect my thoughts over the engine room visit; questions that I had been unable to ask through the excess of noise were now answered.

My presence did not interrupt their social exchange – those not involved in the engineering talk overlooked my occupancy of the port-side table. Neither did my being there overshadow a report to the Chief from Davey and Gunning on work they had carried out below decks. Apparently, while at Hull, there had been a mechanical problem with one of the two cargo lifts on the lower 'tween deck. Over the past two days each of these men had spent several hours stripping part of the hydraulic system to replace worn seals; the lift had to be serviceable for the turnround at Helsinki.

"I'll come down at eleven and we'll give her a final workout," was Clive Buchan's reply to their confirmation of 'job completed'.

"As you can see an engineer's lot does not start and finish in the engine room alone. Whether it be winches, stern doors, cranes or lifts they all need attention at some time or other. With the ship being at sea most of its life that is when such work is carried out. We have strict maintenance schedules to which, if at all practically possible, we adhere regardless of the position of the ship."

Soon after eleven I made my way across a rain-soaked after-deck to join the party of engineers below. Retracing my route from whence I first came aboard, I descended three stairways to find myself within the ship's cavernous belly. It was a gaunt lifeless place. Walls of steel, deck of steel, roof of steel and, not the least, more solid than a house, two towering dungeon doors rammed tight across the stern. Aftermost a cold track-mark deck shook involuntary at the thrusting of the screws directly below. This vibration rang throughout the wide tunnel of the lower 'tween deck. Augmented with a ceaseless roar from the nearby engines, it set up an undying metallic thunder that equalled any severe bashing of an empty drum. Yet this cargo hold was far from empty. Packed lanes of low-load 'Mafi' trailers bearing either secretly sealed containers or inanimate shapes of British-made machinery were lashed downwards with bar-tight chains.

In a clearing midst this sleeping freight, I watched Buchan work at push button controls. A thirteen metre section of the deck steadily sank to the depths of the lower hold. Along with me at the surrounding guard rail, seeing the lift platform faultlessly sink to the deck below, were a somewhat contented Gunning and Davey. The process of taking the forty-five ton lift to its travel limits was repeated several times. Eventually Clive Buchan, satisfied that the system was functioning correctly, came over to compliment his engineers. In doing so he asked John Gunning to make a final check when the lift was operating under load while at Helsinki.

My morning spent touring the ship's innards was concluded by a brief look at the rudder mechanism. Following Paul Davey down a vertical ladder sited near the stern doors, I entered a deep-seated compartment where one could hardly stand upright. Much of this claustrophobic place was filled with a vertical mandrel on which the rudder pivoted and the hefty arms that activated this movement. Davey was there to carry out a routine inspection. In doing so he wasted no time. Here again the noise level was explosive – away from the main engines it must have rated one of the noisiest areas aboard ship – not a place to linger, particularly when, several decks above the smoke-room bar was now open for lunchtime beverages!

*

Settled in the port corner of the bridgehouse, I gazed aimlessly out over a rain and spray drenched weather deck into an everlasting fog. Though the two navigators stationed there knew our exact position relative to the Finnish capital, for all I could see we could have been approaching New York, Sydney or Hong Kong. It was not a time for questions so I quietly penned down the bridgehouse activity until we berthed mid-afternoon at Helsinki's West Harbour. Extracts from my notes read thus:

85

12.45   Bridge manned by Captain and Second Officer. Course – 060
        Speed - 18.5 knots. Distance to Helsinki pilot – 20 miles.
        Visibility – approx 200 yards. Rain has ceased. Ship on
        autopilot - rolling steadily.
        Brazendale in subdued mood finishing tray lunch that has been
        placed on drop-leaf table at the starboard bulkhead. Elworthy
        peering deeply into radar console. Two of the three radar
        consoles are fitted with daylight masks.

12.50   Radio Officer Roy Caple enters through inner door bearing
        message which he takes to Brazendale at the chart table.
        Similarly, steward enters with coffee tray for the two men on
        watch and quickly stacks remnants of Brazendale's lunch –
        within seconds he has gone.

13.00   Visibility slightly improved. Brazendale dons peaked hat, slides
        open starboard bridgehouse door and scours binoculars into
        mist from bridge wing. Shortly he returns to radar screen.
        (Obviously there are other ships close at hand responding to our
        radar beams but not physically in view.)

13.10   Visibility back to 200 yards. Brazendale sips coffee that now
        must be cold. Arranged rendezvous with pilot – 14.00.
        Elworthy rings Bo'sun to have flags hoisted. Shortly A.B.
        arrives at starboard door – Elworthy hands him rolled-up flags
        – including large Red Ensign and Finnish courtesy flag.

13.20   Clive Buchan arrives on bridge – checks engine revs, speed
        through water and then stands at the side of the Master who is
        yet again at the radar screen. Fog is now dense and rain
        sheeting down. Ship still rolling gently. Buchan holds short
        conversation with Brazendale then picks up spare binoculars
        and scans into fog that is by now almost engulfing our bow.

13.25   Elworthy at chart table calls over to Brazendale that we have
        reached position to change course. Captain adjusts autopilot to
        effect 15 degree port turn. Now on 045. Fog eases considerably.
        We sight small freighter to starboard, it is also heading for
        Helsinki but due to our superior speed it is soon overhauled.

13.30   Distance to pilot -7 miles. Distance to Helsinki – 10 miles.
        Speed - 18.5 knots. Course – 045. Rain has stopped and sky is
        brighter than at any other time today. Fog continues but clear
        patches becoming more frequent. Fog siren still issuing two-

minute warnings from its fore-mast perch.

13.40   Brazendale asks Elworthy for a helmsman. Elworthy rings Bo'sun for an A.B. and informed him that the pilot boat will come along the port side.

13.43   Helmsman arrives – makes careful study of compass display and asks if he has to hold 045.
Brazendale: "Easy to port!"
Though there is no skyline on which to follow the steady swing one can physically feel the ship pulling round onto a more northerly heading.
Brazendale: "Midships! - Steady!"
Helmsman : "Steady 005 sir!"

13.50   Fog is very thick. Brazendale brings engines down from 10 to 5 ahead. He moves constantly between the three radar displays, and then turns to Elworthy. "Give pilots a call please."
Elworthy responds: "Baltic Enterprise –Harmaja pilot – we shall be at your station in ten minutes."
Reply over V.H.F. loudspeaker: "Thank you Baltic Enterprise – understand ten minutes."

13.55   Fog is very thick. Brazendale briefly looks at radar then returns to controls and reduces to 2 ahead. Now muted and enclosed within a thick blanket of sea fog, ship ambles lethargically forward at the will of a grey cross swell.

14.00   Brazendale and Elworthy constantly scanning for pilot boat through radar and binoculars.
Brazendale: "How does she head?"
Helmsman: "005"
Progress – dead slow.

14.03   Gulls loom over weather deck as though to guide us through fog – for siren booms out and they hasten away
Brazendale: "005!"
Helmsman: "005."
Progress – dead slow.

14.05   Red and white beacon appears close down starboard side, another shows up to port. Rocky islet topped with lighthouse looms out of mist a few points to port. This is Harmaja!
Brazendale: "007!"
Helmsman: "007."

Brazendale: "Have you got someone standing by for the pilot?"
Elworthy: "Yes sir."

14.06   Pilot launch painted cream and red powers out of the mist on port side. Making for pilot door it livens up the grey water with a half-circle of foaming wake. Brazendale asks Bernard Elworthy to go down to the weather deck to meet the pilot.

14.07   Launch alongside – dwarfed by our ship's towering hull. Pilot climbs rope ladder and is helped through door. Visibility improves considerably – long string of islands beyond Harmaja now in view.
Brazendale from port wing: "015!"
Helmsman: "015."
Entering bridgehouse Brazendale moves engine controls to 5 ahead both.

14.09   Elworthy and pilot enter bridgehouse. Brazendale greets pilot with customary hand-shake. He is a fair-haired man of medium build donned in waterproofs. Walking into bridgehouse he calls helmsman: "Port easy – midships – steady!" His English is surprisingly clear. For the first time in several hours the pressure is momentarily off the Captain – he walks over to me and comments on the irony of the climatic conditions: "Incredible isn't it; as soon as the pilot steps aboard that damned fog leaves us; should have picked him up two hundred miles back!"

14.10   Now abeam of Harmaja Island – apart from lighthouse can see number of low buildings on rocky site – this is the pilot station. Fog has cleared – hazy sunshine breaking through. Helsinki waterfront, distance 3 miles, appears on skyline between nearby islands.

14.12   Elworthy on internal phone informs first and third officers that we shall be docking in 15 minutes.
Pilot: "Port ten!"
Helmsman: "Port ten."
Brazendale now uncovering engine controls on port wing.

Recognisable on our starboard side was Suomenlinna – this being an 18th century sea fortress that links a group of five islands. It makes a fine seaborne introduction to Finland's capital – its rugged stone ramparts rear from grassy knolls and granite shores to guard the entrance to Helsinki's South Harbour. The fortress was built under Swedish rule. On completion it was considered to be impregnable but, haplessly, was belittled by the bombardment of Anglo-French forces in 1855 during the Crimean War.

I well remember seeing, on the television series 'Royal Heritage', coverage of Queen Elizabeth II's arrival at Helsinki during her summer visit of 1976. The Royal Yacht Britannia sailed alongside Suomenlinna's eastern shores. Here, bathed in brilliant sunshine, ranks of military guards were stood to attention. From the after decks of their ship, Her Majesty and Prince Phillip acknowledged a salute fired from cannon at the fortress walls. The Royal Yacht berthed at South Harbour, this being a fitting location to conduct such a visit. I feel certain it was an occasion that the royal couple would long remember.

Through the dramatic change in the weather our arrival at Helsinki was to exceed all expectations. Our destination was the commercial docks of the West Harbour, consequently the pilot guided the ship past the south-west shores of Suomenlinna; its grassy slopes were dotted here and there with families taking an afternoon break from the city. As we paced nearer to our destination a grey and white ribbon of majestic buildings, freshened by the departed rain, spread across our northern seaboard. Some were a distance from the waterfront but crowning this elegant façade was the green-domed tower of Helsinki's Lutheran Cathedral. It is regularly said that Helsinki should be first seen from the sea, preferably in the summertime. I was fortunate enough to fall into such an introduction.

It is said that Helsinki should be first seen from the sea. Fortuitously, after leaving 200 miles of sea fog behind, our landfall met all expectations.

14.15   Suomenlinna to starboard – pilot calling steerage changes intermittently – "Port five – midships – port five."
Bo'sun and crewmen work on crane releases then walk out to the forward mooring deck. Green replaces Elworthy on bridge.

14.18   Wooded island to port – Helsinki waterfront directly to starboard. Making for industrial area – cranes, sheds and quays. Maclaughlan and two crewmen on aft mooring deck. Pilot following buoyed channel weaves ship tightly first to starboard then to port.

14.20   Brazendale at engine controls. Speed approx. 7 knots. – only a half mile from the shore now.

14.23   Factory complex on peninsula of land directly to starboard. Pilot edges *Enterprise* around this promontory through constant calls to helmsman – "Starboard twenty! – Midships! – Hard to starboard! – Midships!"

The nucleus of Helsinki is sited on a peninsula that spreads itself seawards in a most irregular fashion. It is best described as an island situation with numerous jigsaw-like off-shoots reaching from its central hub – the northern arm being the link with the mainland. West Harbour (Länsisatama) is an inroad stretching the best part of a mile between what appeared to be fingers of reclaimed land.

The pilot's tight starboard turn of ninety degrees had brought our ship into West Harbour facing directly towards the city. Within this cul-de-sac she was eased at less than walking pace towards a clearing amidst a string of ships on our port side. Brazendale, operating from the port wing, was now very much back in command. Using the same dexterity he had shown three days earlier in the confines at Hull, he glided the *Baltic Enterprise* to a standstill angled some twenty degrees to the vacant quay. Now, after more than a thousand miles of open water, we were in an urban environment. Apart from the ships berthed ahead and astern, we were among lines of sheds and cranes; to starboard there were factories displaying the names 'Ford' and 'Volvo'. Ahead the rain soaked rooftops of the city dried under an ever strengthening sun.

At our arrival the quayside seemed to burst into life. Cars and people busied between the buildings and offices. Shore crews at the water's edge looked skywards awaiting our warps. Tractors with flashing lights atop of their cabs were revving in readiness for the assault on our cargo. Officials with clipboards stood by for the moment they could be aboard.

Beneath our stern a broad concrete ramp reached from the main frontage for more than a ship's breadth. Bo'sun Edwards and his men, reacting swiftly to a command from their Captain, occupied themselves with our forward lines – ultimately it was against these warps that Brazendale worked his engines to swing *Enterprise* nearer the quay to face her stern doors at the ramp. Through an Olympic class throw a member of our after-deck crew had the 'monkey's fist' of his heaving line scurrying over the concrete more than twenty feet below. From then on, apart from a few final adjustments by winches and engines we were as good as berthed.

As Brazendale rested the control levers of the ever-willing engines into the zero position, Bernard Elworthy, now stationed on the after-deck, had both stern doors hinging from the vertical. Simultaneously, Peter Green, at the chart table, busied himself with the ship's log. His entry was concluding another short chapter in an encyclopaedia of voyages. Glancing at his wristwatch while gratefully relaxing his frame against the white rail of the port wing, Gerry Brazendale called to his Chief Officer, "Sixty-seven hours to the minute!"

I doubt whether Green heard the Captain voice his satisfaction for there was no reply. As it was he already knew that we had made good time; the ship's chronometer before him read 14.30 precisely.

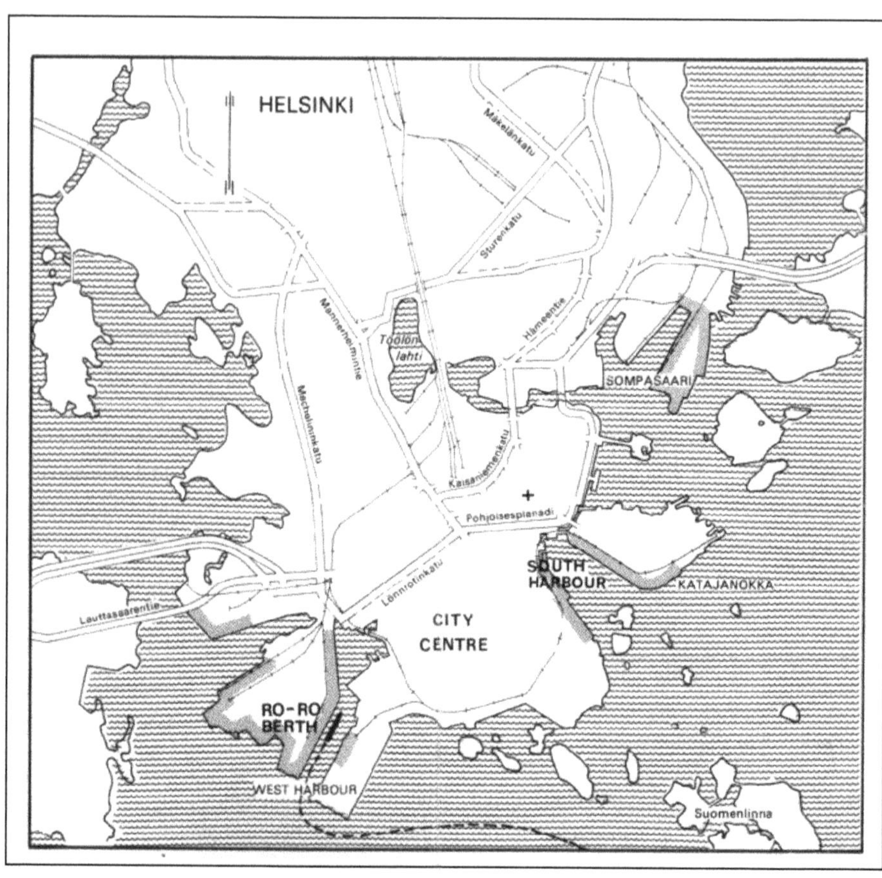

Helsinki city centre is sited on a peninsula of land that spreads itself seawards in the most irregular fashion. It is best described as an island situation with numerous jigsaw-like offshoots reaching from its central hub – the northern arm being the link with the mainland. Our destination, West Harbour (Länsisatama), was along a mile long inlet stretching between industrialised fingers of reclaimed land.

8. Helsinki – A Brief Encounter

At her West Harbour berth, the *Baltic Enterprise* was located less than two miles from Helsinki's central shopping area and principal tourist attractions. But unless for some unforeseen reason we should be delayed in port overnight, for the ship's crew, the city was as remote as the stars. These restrictions created by the rapid roll-on roll-off system did not apply to the crewmen alone. As a round voyage passenger one has to accept whatever opportunity there may be to go ashore, no matter how brief, as a bonus to the sea voyage.

In this instance our ship was to discharge 3,000 tons of miscellaneous ro-ro freight and load approximately 1,000 tons. The ship would be berthed at West Harbour not an hour longer than it would take to complete this process. From the moment the stern doors had been lowered an enthusiastic gang of Finnish dockworkers, our own crew members and a variety of visiting officials had our turnround under way. From the very off the whole ship buzzed with activity – the decks, walkways and accommodation alleyways became alien to the unfrequented places we had come to know.

"How long shall we be staying in Helsinki?" This is a question that had been asked by more than one person during the outward voyage. It had been a question to which no one had a direct answer.

"It all depends on how much freight we have to load there," was the usual reply.

But now along with Bob and Ruth Turnbull I had been assured that the ship would not be sailing for Kotka, its next scheduled call, until some time late evening.

"If this was a conventional freighter I could have promised you at least two days to go ashore," John Garvey said as he handed over our stamped passports. "I suggest that you return no later than 20.30 hours ship's time," were the Catering Officer's farewell words at his office door as the three of us made off for Finnish soil.

Down on the quayside we said our goodbyes to our travelling companions. The Jacksons were packing luggage into the boot of their Cortina. Likewise Philip Rowe's truck had been driven ashore – we found him somewhat impatiently pacing around awaiting final paperwork clearance.

Through the foresight of John Garvey we had been offered a lift into the city by a young Finn. He had been to the ship to deliver a portfolio of documents from the Helsinki agents. Our short journey in the tiny Datsun was one of speed. Although our chauffeur assumed a style in keeping with the Finnish dynasty of world famous rally drivers he gave an unbroken commentary on the shore side features that whizzed past. On our right hand side was a large basin of shimmering water fronted by several buildings similar to very tall aircraft hangars.

"It is here that Finland's famous icebreakers are built," our driver proudly announced.

Later I learned that the sheds formed part of the giant Wartsila shipyard where, along with icebreakers, the Finns built all categories of ships for home and abroad. Very much on the 'home' front there was the building of the *Finnjet* in 1976.

None too soon the Datsun screeched to a halt at a set of city centre traffic lights. "This is where I leave you," we were unexpectedly advised.

Marooned on a central reservation between two lanes of horn-rasping vehicles we stood our ground until the traffic lights granted us our freedom. Here I parted company with the Turnbulls in their search for a nerve-steadying cup of tea. For my part, I had to find one or two small gifts for my family before the shops closed. Nearby was Stockmanns, a complete department store taking up most of a city block on Aleksanterinkatu. Being Finland's largest retail establishment it made a convenient port of call to find traditional Finnish wares.

Helsinki has not always been Finland's capital. Nor have the Finns always enjoyed autonomous government; in terms of independence Finland is a relatively young country. Under many centuries of Swedish rule, Turku, a hundred miles or so to the west, was deemed to be favourably close to Stockholm and thus ideally situated to be the Finnish capital. It was only after many wars between Sweden and Russia on Finnish soil that, in 1809, Finland was ceded to Russia. As a Grand Duchy of Russia the seat of government was established at Helsinki. Consequently, Tsar Alexander I commanded that Helsinki should be rebuilt in accordance with its new status as capital. Through an extensive building programme, highlighting the classical style of the period, a city of great dignity evolved.

Exactly one hundred years later the Grand Duchy was dissolved and Finland became part and parcel of the Russian Empire. It was not until the Russian revolution in March 1917 that the ultimate ideal of independence came within the grasp of the Finnish people. During this time of political upheaval they brought pressure to bear and returned to exercise powers belonging to days of the Tsar. The Russian government of the day raised no objection and on 6 December 1917 Finland proudly declared her independence.

Through the regular conflicts between Sweden and Russia and the periodic sequence of rebuilding, the face of present day Helsinki is relatively modern. With a population approaching one million, the residential suburbs reach away from the peninsula site. Several islands have been linked to the mainland by a road system that brings the city centre within a fifteen minute journey.

Mannerheimintie is Helsinki's main thoroughfare. It is a broad, tree lined avenue that arrows directly through the central area and out to the main Turku road. The street is named in memory of Marshal Gustaf Mannerheim, Finland's military and political hero (Finland's equivalent to Britain's Winston Churchill) who fought to accomplish much during the infant years of independence; he became Finland's president in the twilight years of his life. On his death in 1951 Marshal Mannerheim was given a full state funeral after lying in state in Helsinki Cathedral for three days. Fronting onto Mannerheimintie is a wide variety of places to interest Helsinki's many foreign tourists – the House of Parliament, National Museum, Finlandia Hall and the Olympic Stadium.

On leaving Stockmanns I trudged northwards along Mannerheimintie in prospect of including a glance at some of the aforementioned attractions within a self-styled whirlwind city tour. Arriving at the imposing frontage of the granite-built Parliament House I took stock of my time schedule and, allowing a space to visit South Harbour and Senate Square, abandoned the idea of venturing any further from the centre.

Across the broad highway an equestrian statue of Marshal Mannerheim stood proudly on a high plinth in front of the General Post Office, while further along at the Central Station I stood back to digest the work of Eliel Saarinen. This massive creation was a product of the early 20th century when red granite was the fashion in Helsinki's building programme. My visit to the station was by way of an errand. In the giant main hall I found the Finnish equivalent to W.H. Smith where, at the counter, "English newspapers" was my request. I was offered two or three Sunday papers for which on my return to the ship the crew were most appreciative.

Senate Square, hailed as one of the finest squares in northern Europe, must be Helsinki's principal architectural showpiece. Designed by Engel exclusively in the 'Empire' neo-classic style, this perfectly balanced precinct looks as though it came straight out of a fairytale. The buildings aren't there just for their good looks. Such important places as the Government Palace and the University occupy the east and west flanks respectively.

In marked contrast to Helsinki's thronged commercial streets and boulevards, Senate Square was almost devoid of parked cars or moving traffic or its auditory retort. Besides myself and a central bronze statue of Tsar Alexander II there was but a handful of people there to record the special beauty of these buildings in the light and shade of a semi-incandescent sun.

One of the four elegant neo-classic style buildings that front onto Senate Square.

The Cathedral, dominating the square from a granite rock base thirty feet above it, rose skywards like a giant iced cake with green-coppered domes for added decoration. Within its snow-white walls the hush was most intense. Here I could not help reflecting back to my visit to the ship's engine room that very same day – surely this must have been the extreme in audio contrasts. Compared to British Gothic masterpieces, the interior was distinctly plain, yet despite this smoothness, nonetheless eminent.

Helsinki Cathedral.

Through its comparative modernity Helsinki is often titled the 'Daughter of the Baltic'. At the west end of the Market Square I was confronted with a circular fountain featuring a nude beauty named Havis Amanda. After its creation in 1908 it was adopted as Helsinki's 'Sweetheart'; she is said to symbolise the youthful city rising from the sea.

Here I was in sight and sound of South Harbour – the prominence around which present day Helsinki was founded. Perhaps the water's edge is an unusual site for a market place, but forming the northern limit of the harbour there was no mistaking its importance to traders or buyers of both sea and land harvest. Facing the Market Square and across the sparkling water were many fine buildings – among them the Town Hall, the Supreme Court and further along the ceremonially guarded President's Palace. Between these buildings and the waterfront, the cobbles are lined with neat rows of traders' stalls. Excepting Sunday the market is run each morning; a scene of colour and relentless activity amid eye-catching displays of fruit, flowers, vegetables and seafood. At evening time the thronged atmosphere is long past – strolling the bare and empty cobbles with a small colony of white gulls (now 19.00hrs local time) I relied on imagination to capture the feeling of it all.

In contrast the harbour was busied with all manner of craft. Apart from being the embarkation point for Suomenlinna and other outlying islands, which the Finns ply to and from relentlessly in the summer months, South Harbour is the terminal for the large passenger ferries (including the *Finnjet*) that link Helsinki with Sweden and Germany.

Helsinki's South Harbour was a hive of activity. Double-ended ferries depart here for the short crossing to the island retreat of Suomenlinna.

I took to the west side of the harbour, favouring a steady walk along Helsinki's scenic waterfront as a means of a route back to the ship. Bowing from South Harbour to the main foreshore, the esplanade (Ehrenstromintie) carried me in view of the many off-shore islands and islets. The prospect was more of a quiet and unspoilt lakeside than that of a far reaching sea. There are more than 30,000 islands around Finland's seaboard that, in forming a natural barrier against angry seas, provide an idyllic playground for boat owners and nature lovers alike. Allowing for the fact that the bulk of the country's population lives around the shoreline, it comes as no surprise that the Finns take to the water as the British take to the roads. That Monday evening was no exception, for beyond the promontory around which I strolled the shimmering sea was littered with small craft – yachts at anchor, motor boats weaving around the islands and dinghies coaxing the fickle breeze.

Jetties for carpet washing were a public amenity at Helsinki's waterfront.

Facing the sea at that stage was a blend of fine buildings (this was a district where various foreign embassies are located) and the broad leafed woodlands of Kaivopuisto Park. This greener part of the city attracts Helsinki's many joggers – a number of such, both male and female, young and old, I met en route. Then there were more boat landings, small marinas and an intriguing type of jetty. Upon these square pontoons were three or four benches where both men and women scrubbed away at rugs, carpets and the like. These floor-covering 'laundrettes' are a facility provided each summertime at all Finnish waterside towns. This idea stems back many generations and today, with a high percentage of townspeople living in flats, is one that is put into full use.

Having walked some distance and still out of striking distance I chose to take a taxi back to the ship. Here the non-English speaking manager of a waterfront filling station was of great assistance. On my stressing "Taxi – *Baltic Enterprise*" he jovially acknowledged with arm movements emulating a ship at sea then picked up the telephone. A large black Volvo pulled up on the forecourt within minutes.

The ship was so surrounded in activity I had to pick my way through workers and vehicles both ashore and aboard. Sheepishly I crept into the Dining Saloon in hope of a belated dinner. It was near 19.00 ship's time and I was aware that the usual assembly would have broken up. However good fortune smiled upon me for I was not alone – Gerry Brazendale and Peter Green were sat together at the centre table. Having been greeted with the usual pleasantries I sensed that something was afoot.

Back at West Harbour the ship was in the midst of a turnround.

"Had a good run ashore – how was Helsinki?" Brazendale asked.

I gave a much abridged version of my flying visit commenting that I would have preferred to have seen the capital at a more leisurely pace.

"Well it looks as though you will be seeing a little more of Finland than you expected." Peter Green's contribution came as the steward placed a dish of salmon salad before him.

At my arrival the Captain and Chief Officer had been going through a revised schedule that had been received shortly after docking that afternoon. Due to a re-allocation of cargoes our running sister, *Sirius*, had been re-routed off her west coast service and was heading for Helsinki in our wake. Following our Tuesday call at Kotka we were to head for the west coast of Finland to take aboard *Sirius*'s England bound cargo. This meant additional calls at Turku and Mäntyluoto involving four hundred miles of coastal sailing, the ship loaded to its limit and a thirty-six hour delay to our return to England.

As fore-mentioned the Finanglia services were at the time operating with one ship out of service. During the summer holiday period, Finnish exports are at their lowest. Consequently this proves to be the most convenient time to carry out annual dry-dock surveys. At that very moment we were taking aboard London bound freight for the absent *Baltic Progress* in addition to our shipment. This deviation was already adding one extra day to the usual eight day round voyage. Now that this had been stretched further it was a bitter pill to swallow for some of the crewmen who originally hoped to start leave the coming weekend.

Brazendale had become philosophical over the matter. "The dickens of this regular ferrying is that you begin to organise your life around its schedules. Really we should not depend on the ship adhering to a strict timetable but at some time or another we are all guilty of this. When something untoward happens involving even the shortest delay it can upset your whole domestic arrangements. Had we been deep-sea this temporary diversion would have gone more or less unnoticed – sometimes, on such a voyage, an infringement of this nature could be rectified by speeding up turnrounds later on. With short haul ro-ros being run at optimum output there is no way that two lost days can be recovered. The only way to bring her back on time is to readjust the schedule."

From a passenger's point of view there could be no grievances. In this instance both the Turnbulls and I were more than happy to accept a more comprehensive cruise around Finland than originally planned. Indeed Bob and Ruth had decided to disembark at Purfleet instead of Hull returning home more or less as planned. Through my city wanderings I had been last to be informed; with a much appreciated meal inside me I joined a rather dismayed queue of crewmen at a quayside telephone box waiting to advise families of our delayed return.

*

Whatever class or type of ship, the responsibility for the day-to-day administration of the deck department rests on the head of the Chief Officer. Assisted by the Second and Third Officers he is answerable to the Captain for the operational efficiency of all deck gear, the discipline, training and deployment of crew and, all important, ensuring that the cargo is loaded, stowed and discharged safely. It was in the latter of these executive duties that Peter Green was engaged for most of that evening. On the news of our extended voyage he and the local cargo superintendant had to rearrange the original loading plan.

Sited at the after end of the 'tween decks and overlooking the stern door aperture was a small control room. While working cargo, one of the three deck officers was to be found there. Seated by the control cabin's plate glass window, Green watched an intermittent flow of 'tugmaster' hauled containers roll aboard. At his right hand an array of coloured lights filled a bulkhead mounted circuit board. As the ship lay at the quayside it was important to keep her on a level plane. Green explained: "Should the ship be listing while being loaded, the stern doors, being angled to the ramp, would be under tremendous stress resulting in serious damage."

Checking the ship's attitude as a heavily burdened trailer passed beneath the window, he reached to the illuminated control panel and activated the transfer of ballast from one area to another. The lights on the panel indicated the route along a network of arteries on which the water ballast was being carried.

"The fingertip control of trimming ship allows a substantial margin of flexibility when distributing the load. Theoretically we could almost fill the starboard freight lanes and still balance the level while the port side was empty."

102

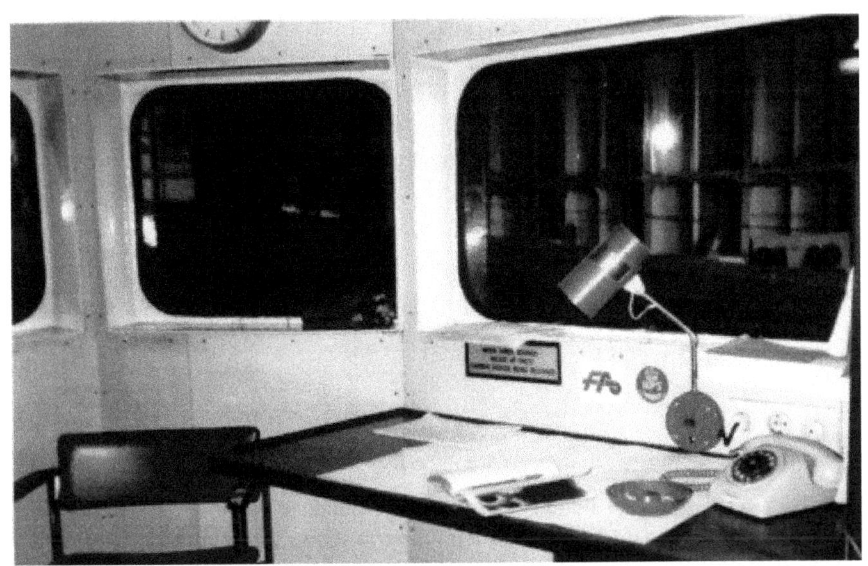

The Freight Deck Control Room

At that stage an oncoming chain of containers was either being transferred by deck lift to the lower hold or lifted through an opened hatch to be deposited on the weather deck by the ship's own gantry crane. At the lower level Willie Maclaughlan presided while the Finnish riggers cranked the lashing chains bar taught. Bernard Elworthy carried out similar duties in the fading Helsinki daylight above.

What were the containers carrying? Their gaunt steel sides displayed nothing but shipping lines' names and a series of registration marks. Peter Green was quick in blocking my inquisitiveness. "Scanning through the cargo manifest it looks as though there could be everything from machinery to mackintoshes! General cargo is the simplest answer to your question. Tomorrow we shall be in the paper business. Kotka thrives round its sawmills and allied industries – we berth almost on the doorstep of a large pulp mill."

Apart from the bustling of the 'tugmaster' tractors, the quayside had been busied throughout by a fleet of articulated oil tankers. Each in turn, dwarfed by our soaring hull, levelled alongside and discharged its load through hefty pipes that disappeared through the port side bunkering door.

"We shall be lucky to be away by midnight," Peter Green said during the evening when it was obvious that the re-allocation of cargo space was slowing the loading process. Indeed at 23.50hrs we watched a low-slung Mafi trailer decked with two 40-foot containers rumble aboard; this concluded our Helsinki commitment.

The 'cut away' starboard side of the 1:100 scale builders' model of *Baltic Enterprise* housed at the National Maritime Museum clearly shows the ship's four freight deck levels. (National Maritime Museum.)

Despite the sustained efforts of all concerned we did not cast our mooring lines from the quays of West Harbour until 00.30hrs ship's time. Amid a flood of illumination both from aboard and ashore the *Baltic Enterprise* eased sedately from the waterfront. Heading stern first towards the darkness, Gerry Brazendale eased the bulky ro-ro quietly past sleeping ships, factories and wharfs. At the main waterway she began to waken to the occasion – her bow was turned to face the moonlit channel and, under the guidance of a local pilot, we began to retrace our steps back to Harmaja Island.

Once away from the high-pylon illumination at the dockside the beauty of the night sky became the captivating element. In the not too distant north the summer sun had barely set before rekindling to the new day, yet, in stark contrast above and beyond to the southern extremities of the Baltic Sea, a powerful moon had radiated an ice-cold phosphorescence amid a dark and starry sky.

While slowly drawing further from the twinkling lights of Helsinki's majestic waterfront, the promise of seeing night and day meeting in one sky became an ongoing realism. Across the city skyline rose an arc of light simulated within a vignette of prismatic colours. From a burnt-orange haze (against which the asymmetrical shapes of the stately buildings were silhouetted) the halo climbed through a delicate turquoise to a brilliant royal blue; directly overhead a more darkened blue was burnished by the moon's silver lustre. The aurora not only captured the undivided attention of the romantics aboard (a small group of onlookers at the port rail included Bob and Ruth Turnbull, Clive Buchan, Peter Green and John Gunning), even the heads of the most hardened seamen were occasionally turned from their work on the mooring decks to marvel at its beauty.

Soon the ship turned her head to the south, leaving Suomenlinna on our port quarter. With several islands fronting the Helsinki backdrop the scene became more compulsive. The spread of water that now lay astern, ruffled only by our gathering wake, became a mirror to the overhead spectacle.

"I have seen this effect on many occasions but never more beautiful than this." The statement came in accented English from our temporary navigator who, on completion of his assignment, was making for the lower decks.

While the ship hovered to accept the tiny pilot launch Harmaja lay close to starboard. Its squat lighthouse set amid the rocks steadily beamed forth alternate red and white warnings. For me this marked the culmination of a brief but memorable visit to the Finnish capital – a visit indelibly etched within the framework of an idyllic departure.

With the pilot boat on its way to the island base, Brazendale pushed his engine controls meaningfully to the ten ahead reading. Above, responding in a businesslike manner, the exhausts thrust sparks of ignited soot into the night air. In four short words the Captain spelled out our immediate mandate – "We go to Kotka."

9. Kotka for Breakfast

I woke to a silence to which I had not been accustomed aboard ship. On looking out I discovered that we were lying quietly at the Kotka ro-ro berth, brightly illuminated in the early morning sunlight. During the early hours *Enterprise* had devoured around ninety sea miles arriving at Finland's largest export harbour complex before the working day had dawned. Until such times as the cargo would start to 'roll' the ship was settled down to a rare interval of inactivity. Those who had stood watch through the night had grasped the opportunity of an unscheduled sleep – short as it would be. As for myself, I was soon dressed and treading lightly along the deserted alleyways en route for the lower decks.

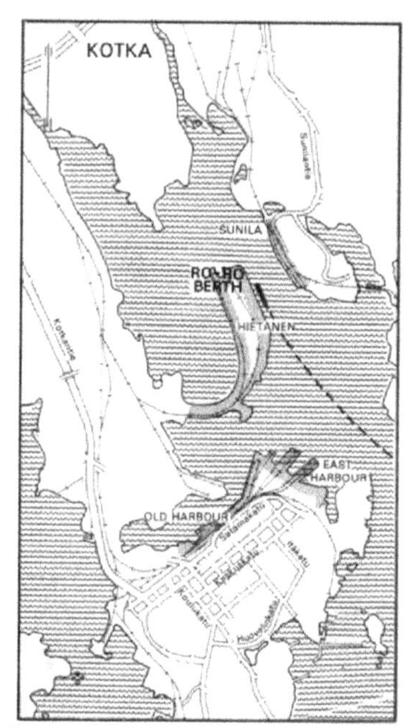

Often ro-ro berths are a considerable distance from town - Kotka was no exception.

Though I had been warned that our stay at Kotka would be brief I was determined to visit the town; even though this meant rising at an unsocial hour. In keeping with the general run of ro-ro berths the Kotka terminal was a considerable distance from the main hub of the town. Lucklessly, as was expected, transport at that time of day was not in abundance. Subsequently, putting my best leg forward for the three mile hike, I stole through the opened stern doors on a pre-breakfast expedition.

At the berth directly ahead of *Enterprise,* also with stern doors open for loading, was a sister ship from the Finnish side of the operation – the green hulled *Orion.* She had arrived at Kotka several hours ahead of ourselves and was scheduled to depart for Felixstowe at midday.

Leaving the twin ships awaiting their freight I moved away from the quayside and viewed the surroundings. The harbour (Hietanen Satama) was one of Kotka's recent port expansion projects. It was sited on what was once a close-shore island. A wide sweeping bight of new founded land carried a link road and railway towards the suburbs. Working my way along this concrete strip I was confronted by a steady flow of traffic heading for the docks – the working day was about to start. With thoughts of the impending turnround and the ship's departure I was induced to lengthen my stride. For such an early hour the sun was exceptionally hot – my wristwatch was barely reading 06.00!

From the elevated viewpoint at Haukkavuori the whole plan of Kotka opened up.

Kotka, not usually projected as a key point on the tourist map, is an unassuming coastal town of some 35,000 inhabitants that radiates an air of confident progress through a hardworking background. It was developed around two islands at the mouth of the Kimi River. The islands are now permanently joined to the mainland by a series of road bridges and earthworks. The hub of the town is based on the most seaward area, this being Kotka Island.

My brisk stride hastened me along an irregular route that moved from the dock area through a residential suburb of variable housing and across the Kotka Island link into the town centre. Here were essentially modern streets favourably studded with broad-leafed trees that emitted the fragrance of the morning. I was pleasantly surprised to find an abundance of green areas. My meandering soon revealed tree-shaded boat harbours, playing fields with all the attendant facilities, and parks and gardens where women had already started sweeping the footpaths.

Unlike Helsinki it was not a town of architectural gems. Largely due to the ravages of war Kotka had little to show of its illustrious past. Though this historical background is shorter in time than other Finnish towns, it is perhaps of greater interest. Indeed, before the last decades of the 18th century the name Kotka was only related to pasture, fishing waters and burn beaten land. Development of present day Kotka commenced in the 1860s when the industrial revolution led to a massive upswing for Finland's woodworking industry. The utilisation of the Kymi River as a watercourse on which to float logs from the vast upland forests opened the way for the development of sawmills and the installation of a harbour at its estuary. The sawmill and harbour town with its thousands of casual workers acquired a reputation as a form of Finnish 'wild west'. It was a place where the unsavoury recklessness of a 'Klondike' town was rife.

Kotka was not transformed into an orderly community overnight – many decades were to pass before it established complete social reform. A further chapter in Kotka's illustrious history was opened up during World War II when advancing Russian forces subjected the town to almost continuous bombardment. It is said to have been, apart from Malta, the most bombed point in Europe. Post-war reconstruction was extensive; consequently the majority of buildings seen today came into existence within the past few decades.

Prior to departure the shelved volumes at my local reference library had little to offer by way of information about Kotka. It is a place that travel writers regularly describe as an industrial town and port having limited appeal as a tourist centre. However my resolve to see the town did not lead to disappointment. One of the landmarks to which I trudged was the Old Water Tower. This was an octagonal cream-painted building crowned with a turreted lookout post not dissimilar in appearance to an ancient lighthouse. Set high above the trees on the rocky shelf of Haukkavuori, it is recognised as one of the finest view points in southern Finland. It was from there that the whole plan of Kotka opened up.

The empty streets of early morning Kotka led me to the Orthodox Church of St. Nicholas and onwards to the delightful Sibelius Park.

Southwards and likewise to the west the Gulf of Finland was shimmering in the morning light; clearly its islands, skerries and infinite stretches of water give Kotkans a natural playground for water-borne leisure activities. To the north and east occasional tall chimneys set around inroads of placid waters revealed the economic lifeblood of the area. Close at hand and spread among the trees were the municipal and educational facilities of the town. Kotka boasts a variety of vocational training institutes including Finland's most modern navigational school and the country's only stevedore technical institute.

Back in town I walked in the parkland grounds of the Orthodox Church of St. Nicholas. Built in the classical style with a squat tower and dome, St. Nicholas's was one of two principal structures remaining after the days of the Crimean War, the other being the Imperial Fishing Cabin at nearby Langinkoski which was built by the Finnish government at the request of Tsar Alexander III. The Tsar much loved the area, spending regular summer holidays at the cabin in the late 19th century. Regrettably my schedule would not allow for a visit to the cabin – it has been preserved on its island site and opened to the public as a museum.

Soon Kotka seemed to come alive – the market place was a scene of bustling activity. Aside from heavily burdened vans and pick-up trucks, brightly awninged stalls were being erected and decked with all manner of garden produce. The streets were now filled with the sounds of traffic, people hurrying to work and shops opening for the day. Time was now passing quickly and I had to be getting back to the ship. Twice I stopped to ask the way but the use of the English language was not commonplace in Kotka. Nevertheless, on the tree-shaded patio of a modern coffee house I did manage to place an order for a glass of ice-cold milk and on consuming the same swayed the young waitress into telephoning for a taxi.

*

A ship's agent is someone who must be prepared to 'expect the unexpected'. It is his job to arrange for all the requirements a ship may need and any demands made upon him by the master. This can cover a multitude of requests – any hour, seven days a week. Possibly a crew member may need medical attention or the master may need to recharge his float of ready cash or need currency to cover a call on some foreign shore – stores, fresh water, fuel and repair facilities have all to be readily available. On top of this the agent has to be in constant contact with the ship, booking cargo, arranging storage and dealing with all the documentation concerning the cargo, including those demanded by the Customs and Excise. Considering the number of off-beat jobs that can fall in his sphere of operation, arranging last minute dental treatment for a face-sore member of *Baltic Enterprise*'s crew could not have been far out of the Kotka agent's tenure.

Whilst at Kotka, U.K. destined paper was loaded onto the upper 'tween deck.

The huge Sunila wood pulp works looks westwards over Hietanen harbour. It was the quay to the left of the picture where our ship had berthed.

Insignificant as it may be, the discomfort of the cabin steward did delay our 10.30 (ship's time) scheduled departure to the extent of forty minutes. Cargo stowed and engines running, *Enterprise*, poised to take on the 270n.m. coastal run to Turku, had laid at the Hietanen harbour berth ready for sea for almost one hour before the steward (minus one tooth!) stepped aboard.

During that time, Brazendale had impatiently paced between bridgehouse and starboard wing.

From there, unwittingly patting the palms of his hands against the rail-top, he had more than a dozen times looked out over the close-by transit sheds towards the Kotka road. Anxious to get his charge thrusting westwards, he had called his deck crew to their stations shortly after loading had been completed.

The additional voyage to Finland's west coast was an occupational hazard that had to be contended with. For Gerry Brazendale this was the last of a three, round-voyage session – he had been expecting to start leave on arrival at Hull late the coming weekend. Though he had not made it known at this stage, his annual family holiday had been arranged to commence around this timing. With something in the order of thirty-six hours having been added to the voyage he had incurred problems far from the job in hand. Equally, over the past two days he had had but a smattering of sleep and for him the prospect of any substantial rest period over the next two days was none the more encouraging. Now, as though this was not enough, he was being subjected to further frustration through a steward deciding he had toothache.

Moments after Brazendale had curtly asked Peter Green to, "Get on the phone and find out what the hell is happening," a dust-shrouded taxi swung round the sun-kissed sheds and drew to an abrupt halt on the concrete apron way below. With the Captain's eyes firmly glued to the accommodation ladder it was fortunate that the tall young man did not dally on his ascent.

On departing the Hietanen ro-ro berth we leave the *Orion* (far right) in the throes of her turnround for Felixstowe.

Enterprise departing Kotka on a previous occasion.

With the pilot at his shoulder and voicing his usual litany of orders Brazendale hurried the *Baltic Enterprise* from the ro-ro berth. Our mooring flanked the west shore of a deep-water channel that flowed south for a couple of miles where it met up with the principal waterfront. The sister-ship *Orion*, still in the throes of loading, was soon put on our starboard quarter – to port the giant Sunila wood pulp mill that had overpowered the east bank by both its appearance and unfortunate smell quickly fell beyond our now arrowing wake. Ahead, planed and polished as a sheet of glass, the Gulf of Finland again beckoned our ship's tireless energies: such was our departure from Kotka – a restless, sun-baked occasion framed within a backdrop of Finnish industry.

In the heat of the day, visibility had deteriorated as not to allow a lingering onshore view of the town. Not that this disappointed the crew in any way. Apart from the unusually spectacular sky the previous night, hardly any of them warranted a second glance at anything that did not concern navigation. To them the everyday scene had no more significance than the wallpaper at home. For those who cared to look, the Old Water Tower provided our last visual contact with the shore. Its fresh cream-painted walls, gilded in diffused sunlight, disappeared rapidly behind a curtain of sea-haze that closed in all the more as we travelled.

Had we been travelling eastwards out of Kotka we would have soon been sailing in waters of the USSR – the territorial boundary was a mere twenty-five miles away. On such a heading Leningrad would have been looming up ahead by early evening. As things were, with the Kotka pilot on his way back to base, we were leaving longitude 27 east on a heading of 230 degrees with visibility under two miles. Despite the low-level mist, the sun baked our steel decks to the extent that, regardless of footwear, one sensed burning feet.

Along with several hundred tons of freight our call at Kotka had produced two new passengers – Carl and Gillian. They were fortunate young Americans from whom the pressures of time, finance and responsibilities had seemingly escaped. On a random tour of Europe they had worked their way north and east as far as political boundaries would allow. Having friends in London they were now poised for a few days' break before heading for the Mediterranean. Rather than fly to

London in less than three hours they were in their words, 'happy to take a novel way there' in more than three days!

Though Carl and Gill were 'travelling light' and were content to exist from day to day without alternating their mode of dress, a guitar was considered an essential part of their baggage. From Kotka onwards this guitar, in the capable hands of Carl, brought a new lease of life to an often fallible social atmosphere. Long sunny periods became flavoured with mellow tones of folk music drifting from here and there around the upper decks. In the evening the injection of live music prompted a sing-along atmosphere in the smoke room. On leaving Kotka behind, appropriately the tune was, 'We will sail away together'!

The octagonal Haukkavuori Water Tower, which stands sentinel over the town, provided Kotka's farewell landmark.

10. A Damp Turku – then Northwards on Wheels!

Turku is old and traditional and, having the distinction of being the former capital of Finland, holds a prominent place in northern history. Unlike its successor, Turku was never founded; it developed naturally at the crossing of northern trade routes. The very word 'Turku' means a market or trading place. Present day Turku is an active commercial and industrial centre. Food, textile, precious metal and medical industries together with shipbuilding employ about half of the town's population of 160,000 – commerce almost one fifth. Not least of Turku's key points of activity is its well tree-sheltered harbour. It is from here that the modern ferries of the Viking, Silja and Bore Lines continuously manoeuvre to and fro on turnround for either Stockholm or the Finnish ruled Åland Islands.

The ferry scene on our arrival at Turku harbour was living up to its vibrant record. Two 'seal'-logoed Silja and one red-hulled Viking Line ship busied about the quays that fronted the elevated ramparts of the 13th century castle. It was early – 06.30 ship's time, 07.00 local; it was raining – sheeting down to be more precise. The ferries offered the only splash of colour at the waterside. In retrospect the weather situation since leaving Kotka had been a recycle of that encountered while hauling northwards thorough the Baltic two days earlier – sparkling hot morning, sea-hazy afternoon leading to a foggy evening, overnight rain continuing through to a dull wet morning.

*

The 270-mile coastal voyage from Kotka had revealed little of southern Finland. Had visibility been good we would have been treated to fine scenery as we passed and threaded by summer playground islands, boldly marked skerries and foremost promontories of the mainland. Unfairly, for both passengers and navigators alike, this was not to be. Again as the weather thickened and the day wore on, Brazendale spent long hours pondering over the radar and charts with his subordinates on the bridge. During the early hours of Wednesday morning he had brought *Enterprise* to a near halt at the island of Utö – sixty-four miles south of Turku. It was here that we took on the Turku pilot – a short,

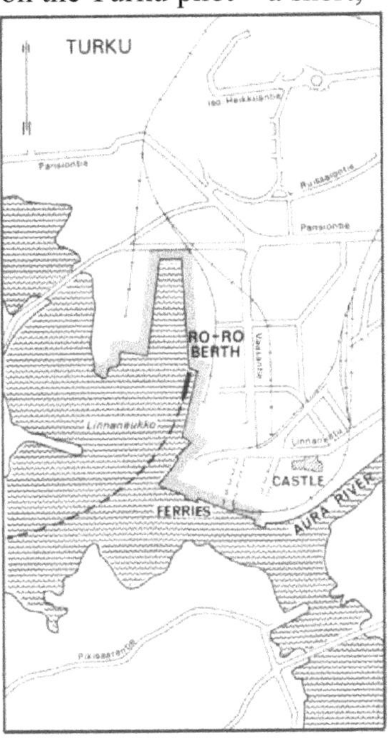

fair-haired man possibly in his late forties who instantly made his presence felt by shaking out his wet waterproofs in the centre of the bridgehouse carpet!

For five hours in half light, fog and rain this man was to guide our ship through the hazard-strewn Turku archipelago. Had it been any other person showering stone-cold water around the bridgehouse at that early hour I feel sure there would have been strong comments from the Captain. As it was I sensed Gerry Brazendale was more than happy to welcome the Pilot to his bridge despite his presumptuous entry.

There was much ferry activity on our arrival in early morning rain at Turku.

The Turku archipelago is claimed to be one of the most beautiful in the world. An outside chance of seeing dawn break over that island group had drawn me from my bed. However, having been advised that it was unlikely that the weather would improve over the next few hours at least I retired until 06.00; by then to watch Turku arise out of the gloom.

By that time we were ghosting between two tree-clothed islands that narrowed the deep-water channel down to a slender river. Aside the tall pines (whose pyramid tops were hung in low mist) small sauna cabins rested at the water's edge. Each had a rickety plank jetty from which near-roasted bathers would plunge naked directly into the cold depths. I was not surprised that there were no such sights to be seen on that occasion. Even the hardy Finns withdraw from taking these 'pleasures' at such an early hour in unseasonal weather!

Soon the channel opened up into a huge, partially tree-fringed basin. At the far side were ferries, cranes and sheds – Turku stood beyond them. There appeared to be an abundance of space to manoeuvre our ro-ro and once more Brazendale, tired as he must have been, brought us accurately to rest at a ramped berth on the main waterfront.

The call at Turku had been made principally to collect empty containers and transport them to Purfleet as weather-deck cargo. The number of containers and trailers on the Finanglia circuit amounted to many thousands. Often some ports run up a surplus of empties and have to feed other bases that are running 'dry'. The loading of the same would not take long and our stay at Turku would be even shorter than that at Kotka. At that, any chance of a 'run ashore' was unlikely – so I began to think. Here I looked at the possibility of making an overland journey while the ship was slowly following the western coastline to Mäntyluoto on the next leg of her voyage. This would allow me a little time in Turku and the opportunity to see something of the Finnish countryside. Erik Nasman from the ship's agents enthusiastically gave me details of coach services to the north so I accepted his offer of a lift to town.

By 11.00 local time, the loading had been completed and the deck crew were at their stations. The customary departure signal bellowed out and from the shelter of his quayside parked car Erik and I watched as the now load banked *Baltic Enterprise* crept from her Turku berth. Her screws bit the water with a vengeance and, as she showed us her twin stern doors, was soon to disappear across the harbour behind a screen of tall pines. It was estimated that she would take between six and seven hours over the 111 miles to Mäntyluoto ('Manty' to those on board); the coach journey that I was to take would amount to three hours. I expected to be reunited with the ship and my companions in time for dinner.

Enterprise departing Turku for her 111-mile haul to Mäntyluoto.

Turku Castle stands on a lawned bank overlooking both harbour and river.

119

Our route to town followed the tree-lined Aura River.

Turku is straddled either side of the Aura River, the mouth of which forms a sizable part of the harbour complex. Our route to town followed in close company with the Aura, this providing the chance of a closer look at the thronging ferry terminals plus, a little further upstream, a string of crane-swathed shipyards. From the tourist's point of view the principal attraction there is Turku Castle. Sited on a lawned banking its solid ramparts and square tower take command of both river and harbour. Having been subjected to a long history of fires, siege, misuse and dereliction the castle was eventually restored to its heyday glory through a twenty year scheme that commenced shortly after the Second World War. Together with a comprehensive historical museum the restored castle offers its visitors a glance at the opulent Renaissance-style rooms in which royalty once dwelt. But the castle is not just a monument to the years gone by, for it is widely used by the people of Turku for all kinds of social and cultural occasions – banquets, wedding receptions and concerts often being held there.

Moored close by the first bridge up river was the Finnish naval training frigate *Suomen Joutsen*. Being on the opposite bank to which we were travelling we could obtain a clear view of her from the broad river concourse. Against a backcloth of green foliage this beautiful square rigger showed her white hull, tall masts and far reaching yard arms in splendid profile.

From the riverside a brief drive along tree-shaded streets took us to the wet, cobblestoned market square. On receiving final directions from Erik, I expressed my thanks, bade farewell and watched his small saloon car disappear among the mid-morning traffic.

Turku Market Square.

Onwards, from a visit to a modern styled bank to replenish my pocket with Finn-marks, much of my short stay at Turku was spent meandering around the city centre – lucklessly trying to avoid the raindrops! Department stores, gift shops and both outdoor and covered markets were heavily thronged with shoppers. Apart from the Orthodox Church at the top of the square, the buildings in that area were mostly modern. Regardless, in standing with the distinction of being a former capital city, Turku generated an air of maturity. Had there been two or three days at my disposal the streets would have led me around a city more than amply furnished with historical tourist attractions.

Swedish is an official language of Finland and is spoken by eight per cent of the country's 4.7 million population. As this 'second' tongue is largely spoken in the south and west regions Turku is one of the Swedish speaking strongholds on the Finnish mainland. I say mainland, for the entire population of the Finnish Åland islands that lie halfway to Sweden speak nothing but Swedish. From my experience I felt Turku was best described as tri-lingual for nowhere (in marked contrast to Kotka) did I find difficulty in communicating with the 'locals'.

Gone lunchtime the clouds began to give way to a lazy sun. The weather forecast had been accurate and it was now time for me to be moving on.

The conductress on the coach was particularly helpful. It appeared that on inter town services these smartly uniformed girls care for their passengers in the manner of an air hostess; helping the aged to their seats, attending to the baggage that was stored in an area free of seats at the rear of the vehicle and announcing our arrival at various points en route. At 14.30 the engine struck up and from my window seat I watched as we whisked by the main railway station and its attendant marshalling yards. Ten minutes later we were drawing away from Turku's suburbs on a well-surfaced highway that undulated towards pine covered countryside. The coach was headed for Pori, a town of some 70,000 inhabitants situated twelve miles from the coast. At Pori I was to change onto a local bus that would take me westwards to Mäntyluoto.

At 130,085 square miles, Finland is one of the largest countries in Europe. It also lies entirely north of latitude of 60 degrees N, which inevitably means long hard winters. These two factors pose a special problem with regard to road transport, for the country's economic stability relies greatly upon a satisfactory year-round transport system. The earliest snowfall comes to the far north in September or October and by Christmas the whole land is under snow. In the south the white carpet can stay anywhere between three and six months at a depth of one to three feet; above the Arctic Circle it lasts between six and eight months. When the snow arrives twenty-five per cent of private motorists garage their cars until spring; the remainder fit winter tyres and for several cold months become proficient at four wheel ice skating!

It is estimated that six million cubic feet of snow and ice are removed from Finland's roads each winter and that over one million tons of sand and salt are spread on them. On the bonus side the frost penetration creates greater load bearing capacity. Often heavy transport can be driven on roads that are classed as unsuitable, soft ground and even swamps. In some cases snowploughs work their way across the ice to inhabited islands in both sea and lakes. At a certain point, on the Gulf of Bothnia between Finland and Sweden, a road is cleared across the ice and substitutes for the ferry service that links the two countries. Throughout this time the country's powerful icebreakers strive around the coast to keep open the south-west ports in all but the hardest weather (Mäntyluoto is considered the northernmost winter port).

The journey to Pori was on well-founded roads that ran straight for miles on end. On some stretches road gangs were busy patching and resurfacing – ominous of the long departed winter's toll. Away from town traffic density was low. At times we could be on open highway without sign of another vehicle. Here and there the coach would pull off the main route onto unsurfaced roads that led to small villages of brightly painted wooden houses. On making its call, which was sometimes to deliver (or pick up) packaged goods rather than passengers, the coach would wend its way back to the trunk road and speed away. At one stage, following one hour of travel, we halted for a break at a combined café, filling station and roadside stores fronted by a shale track that was heavily puddled. I tagged on with the twenty or so passengers who made pilgrimage across the water-borne car park to the café ('Baari' is the Finnish name for such an establishment) and contributed to the depth of red mud left in the doorway. Worthy of note is the Finnish practice of hanging exterior doors to open outwards. This

I understand is to prevent snow falling inside when the door is opened. Personally I see problems here with deep snow and high winds!

The bus service northwards to Pori carried both passengers and parcels.

Through the coach window the countryside seemed generally low lying – in some places decidedly swampy. There were coniferous trees; there had to be, it would not have been Finland without them. Yet it was not the virile forestry as found in the vast upland regions that provide for fifty-five per cent of the country's total exports. The glades of pine, spruce and fir which spread their way down to the roadside were purely characteristic of the area – pleasant woodland of more visual and recreational value rather than of use to a vigorous industry.

Similar in meaning were the occasional stretches of water which offered quiet relief to the green landscape. This was not part of Finland's Lake District; literally we were far from it. Eight per cent of the country's surface area is covered by water and this is concentrated within a vast interior region where lakes are counted in their thousands. I was more than conscious that the small lakes and pinewoods seen that afternoon were only an entrée to the true Finnish landscape; yet without them the journey would have been all the poorer.

On face value there was nothing ostentatious about Pori. Its unglamorous town centre buildings conformed to a certain uniformity generally accepted as the norm when away from the main tourist centres. For me places like Pori (and Kotka) exemplified the backbone of the Finnish ego. Honest hardworking industrial communities with a determination to progress regardless of all adversity. It would be fair to say that Pori has had its share of adversity, for, since being founded in 1558 at the mouth of the Kokemäenjoki River, the town had been ravaged by war and burned many times. Having been devastated by fire in 1852 an extensive rebuilding plan was made and this contributes to the town's present day character. One of the features of that period from which Pori still benefits is a group of riverside houses that are claimed to be one of the country's loveliest architectural sights.

*

The service bus to Mäntyluoto roared, bumped and rattled its way out of town with barely a handful of passengers. Soon it was amid a flat featureless landscape that provided little more than swampy grazing land for equally miserable looking cattle. This was not one of Finland's high spots, least of all a grand finale to my visit. But when one realises that in years long past much of the area was under the sea one cannot cast aspersions on it. Today Pori is much more detached from the sea than say in 1842 when it boasted the country's largest mercantile fleet.

Few would choose to visit Mäntyluoto unless they had business there. For the tourist there is little other than a straggling village of wooden houses, an old stone pier and a long intriguing name. Once a close-shore island, the area (known to the people of Pori as 'Sea Pori') is now linked as an irregular peninsula of land that lends itself to sea-borne industries. Though open westwards to the Gulf of Bothnia, tree-fringed islands group around the near waters to form what one would describe as a natural harbour.

Mäntyluoto is a place of wide open spaces. Acres of dockland are regimentally linked with railway trucks, timber stacks, oil drums and containers. Unlike many ports the sheds do not crowd the waterfront. Not as though there were many sheds, but what there was lay widely spaced from the ships. The commanding visual factor at Mäntyluoto harbour was not the commercial dock. Large-scale construction of oil rigs and platforms was a booming industry there and effectually dominated the northern skyline.

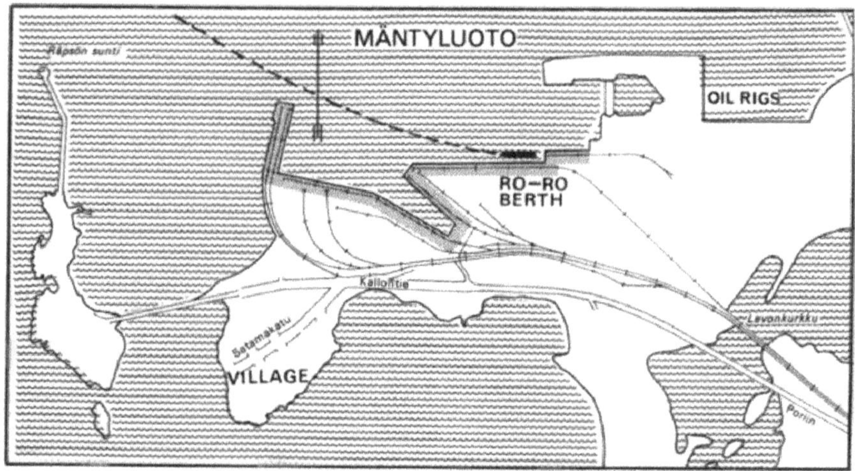

The bus driver motioned that we had reached the terminus. It had to be me he was beckoning, for by now I was the only passenger remaining. I stepped down onto a roadway of compressed shale and waited as he swung the utility vehicle around a marked turning circle and headed back for Pori. He had little alternative; the only option from there was the sea.

As the bus faded into the distance I began to take stock of my new surroundings. Ahead, a line of dockside cranes scribed out the waterfront and that was obviously where I needed to be. As I walked, peering between the massed regiments of railway trucks and containers, I could see the superstructure of two or three ships but certainly nothing answering the description of the *Baltic Enterprise*. Fair enough, the time had only reached 16.45 local, so my ship was hardly due yet – six to seven hours from leaving Turku at 11.00 I had been told. All the same in such an outpost as this I would have felt all the happier had she been moored at the quayside along with what I made out to be two Russian freighters and a small gravel dredger. It was so noticeably quiet; the swishing of grass and the rustle of stray pieces of litter blown by a warm onshore breeze were the only sounds. There were no people either; up to that point I had not met anyone nor in fact seen anyone. It was as if this

126

far flung place had been evacuated.

Cautiously I approached the only building of substance in the immediate area and found it to be the offices of a Finnish shipping company. Inside the hollow foyer I waited at an empty desk for what seemed like an hour. When at long last a middle-aged lady made an appearance behind the desk I was foiled by a language barrier. Communications were bad – non-existent to be more accurate. Eventually two of the good lady's colleagues arrived from back stage and joined in a good-humoured bout of arm gesticulating and ship sketching.

From this session of Anglo-Finnish charades I established that they knew of the ship *Baltic Enterprise* though they had not seen her at Mäntyluoto for many months. They were unaware that she was due to arrive that day but if she were to do so she would use the berth at the far end of the dock approaching the oil rig construction area. Surely the *Sirius* was the ship currently operating on the U.K. service?

Obviously this was not the Finanglia agent's place of business, but the people there had been helpful and I knew in what direction to head. On declining their offer of a seat until such times as they closed for the day, I made off for the corner of the dock where steelwork towers and gantries overshadowed all else.

From what I could see there were two oil rigs under construction at the harbour. One was a five-legged job, nearing completion and already in the water. The other, still in its infancy, was cradled by gigantic cranes, jigs and other miscellany that adorned the yard. This was a thrusting industrial complex which, with its noisy machinery, clattering of metal surfaces and sparking welding torches, contrasted greatly with the still slumbering dockyard. I stared in amazement at the sheer size of the rigs. When on station they present an awe-inspiring sight, but when in harbour their fully revealed enormity is no less than staggering.

Three-quarters of a mile on from the office block, I arrived at what was unmistakably a ro-ro ramp. There were many U.B.C. containers around too and I decided that I had found the berth. Unfortunately it was an empty berth as was the bay and the open water beyond. Sat on a mooring bollard I gazed out to sea and reviewed the situation.

Had I made a grave mistake by leaving the ship? Time was rolling on and still there was no sign of her or any indication that she was about to arrive. Equally none of the few people I had met had any knowledge that *Enterprise* was expected. Could there have been yet another change of orders and she was now heading for London without me? Or could there have been a mechanical failure and she had limped back to Turku? At 61 degrees N, I was further north than at any other time of my life and, apart from a few unused Finn-marks and my passport, I only had what I stood up in. Surely, in the event of my being stranded the agent would have been informed and would send someone to find me. If not? – Peter Green had made mention of a hotel somewhere around here; perhaps I could have a meal there and make a telephone call?

A sight for sore eyes! The *Baltic Enterprise* in silhouette on her late arrival at Mäntyluoto.

While lonely mulling over these probabilities, in what turned out to be a bright and warm summer evening, I became conscious of the dockside awakening from its siesta. Tractor engines were being started, cars were arriving and people were making for the quay. Soon this activity had reached a mini epidemic and it became all too obvious that a ship was expected.

Within minutes the growing apprehension of the last hour or so had been dismissed. From behind the screen of 'Manty's' stone pier, the ship that silently entered the bay was clearly the *Baltic Enterprise*. And what a memorable picture she made too, silhouetted before a diminishing sun while framed between two outlying islands. It was now plain to see that I had arrived at the dock during a work break period that continued until such time as the ship was about to berth. The 'jungle telegraph' had given the alert and now the people who were arriving from nowhere were here to work an evening shift.

*

A remote harbour on the west coast of Finland is not a place one would expect to be savouring the most traditional of all English dishes. Having been prepared by experienced hands the roast beef and Yorkshire pudding proved to be the firm favourite from the dinner menu.

Showered and changed I had joined the assembly which at the sound of the dinner gong had filtered into the immaculately laid saloon. On the Master's instructions, the meal had been delayed thirty minutes. In this instance the docking operation had clashed directly with the usual meal time; clearly this slight change in the domestic schedule was not for the benefit of a stray passenger who had been pondering around the dockside for almost two hours – nonetheless I did find it highly convenient.

Whether it was that we were soon to be homeward bound or simply that we were resting at the quayside I do not know, but this was one of the most convivial and appreciated mealtimes. Much for my benefit and for those being off watch, the conversation revolved around the voyage from Turku. To the accompaniment of structural 'shuddering' induced by the below decks loading, I listened to the reason for the ship's late arrival.

A course had been set by the Turku pilot that carried the ship to the pilot base at Isokari Island. The recovery pilot launch had developed a mechanical failure; consequently it was some time before the pilot could leave the ship. Throughout this time Brazendale had held *Enterprise* stationary through engine manipulations. "We wasted a lot of time there. I was on the verge of bringing the pilot with us to 'Manty' when finally a second boat was sent out to recover him."

From then on, by laying off courses of 314, 015 and 051 degrees, he had worked *Enterprise* up the coast in the most timesaving manner. This route had brought them past some of Finland's finest holiday beaches, but most significant of all she had hauled close to the port of Rauma. It

129

was here at the shipyards of Rauma Repola that, as yard no. 209, the *Baltic Enterprise* was built and completed in 1973.

"Bet you were beginning to sweat a bit when we didn't turn up on time. Great place to be stranded this, 'Manty'. Think of all the theatres, restaurants and night clubs you have here!" John Garvey added to the conversation in his usual light-hearted tone.

Surprisingly, it was not long after dinner that I left the ship for the second time that day. Nils Petterson, an official at the dock, had heard of my interests and came aboard to invite me along to see his home and family. Departure time had been set for midnight, ship's time – I could just squeeze in a two hour visit, so I gladly accepted. We had barely motored five miles when the tall young Finn swung the car off the main road and headed on an unsurfaced track towards a secluded residential estate of individual houses. Nils' home was something rather special on account that he had constructed most of it himself.

Set on an elevated site among tall pines, the timber-built house was of his own split-level design. Indoors the décor and furnishings were very much of the modern Scandinavian style. The principal living area was concentrated on the upper level. Here open planning, solid timber panelling and concealed lighting had been put to full effect. Below was the leisure area which incorporated an indoor sauna cabin with shower and changing rooms. A cosy bar was centred near an open fireplace; also, for the children, a well equipped play area was included. There were utility rooms for laundering and storing bulky winter clothing. Racks contained skis for each member of the family.

Finns rely on a high level of insulation to keep their homes warm through the long hard winters. Often walls have several skins that sandwich layers of specially processed insulation material. Triple glazing had become commonplace – I was told that Finnish government legislation was soon to demand this on all new buildings. Nils' home had all the latest insulation materials installed and an equally efficient heating system that was fed on electricity. Apparently electricity came at a much lower cost in Finland than the U.K.; therefore it was widely used as domestic heating fuel.

After I had been shown over the house, Nils' wife produced coffee, biscuits and Finnish cheese at a candlelit table. My patchy visit to their country was drawing to a close; for this final display of hospitality I was extremely grateful.

11. Workaday Baltic Cruising

We carried from Finland that night an almost capacity load of containerised and trailer stacked freight. Both the weather and after decks were built up with a miscellany of containers. Below, six lanes of heavily burdened slave trailers extended to the stern from both 'tween decks to within feet of the securely rammed stern doors. As an effect of this load *Baltic Enterprise* was now drawing twenty-one feet of water – it was expected that her maximum speed would be reduced by one knot.

On drawing out of Mäntyluoto harbour, all five passengers stood at the after rail. Not that there was anyone to wave goodbye to; we were out of bed purely to witness our departure from that country of the North. It was dark and, for the first time that week, decidedly chilly. Carl's guitar murmured out melancholy chords that registered with the mood of the occasion.

Having slipped our ropes from the quayside bollards, the shore crew had vanished into the night leaving the powerful overhead dockside floodlights to beam down onto lifeless concrete. Nursed further and further from the berth our ship gradually inched her bow towards open water. Soon the old stone pier was slipping beyond the port quarter. We continued at this 'crawl' for a mile or more until the bobbing light of the pilot launch that had fussed about us headed back to shore.

Carl's rendition of 'Yesterday Once More' was suddenly swamped by the chant of thunder that ripped out of the funnel top. Simultaneously, despite the blackness, the dark water beneath our stern was transformed into a foaming mass. Slowly Mäntyluoto's floodlit dockland diminished into an eerie glow; the courtesy flag was lowered. Finland was gone – we were homeward bound.

*

By early morning the chart showed that we had carved 120 miles south-westwards across the Gulf of Bothnia and come to within twelve miles of the Swedish coast. This was the first leg of a 700-mile run down the Baltic that would take an estimated 40 hours. For much of the first half of that voyage we would be sailing 100 miles to the west of our outward course. Later in the day this new route would carry us southwards along the west coast of Gotland, the Baltic's largest island.

Having completed loading at Mäntyluoto the ship was near to her deadweight limit on the 1,200 mile homeward leg of the voyage.

The ship's model projects the ease of access afforded through the twin stern doors. Along with astute management, both shipboard and ashore, this contributed to the speedy turnrounds achieved at our four ports of call. (National Maritime Museum.)

In the meantime, having turned to port onto 144 degrees at the Grundkallen Light, we spent the breakfast hour slipping between Sweden and the Finnish Åland Islands. Said to contain some 6,000 islands the Åland group links with that of Turku. Mariehamn, the capital, is situated at the south-west corner of the staggered 30-mile long main island. It is to there that ferries from both neighbouring shores bring many thousands of holidaymakers each year. One of Mariehamn's main tourist attractions is a maritime museum that features the famous windjammer *Pommern*.

This was to be a day of plain sailing, a day free of pressing commitments and unexpected diversions. Having been given a loose rein, the ship had settled to the task of eating up the Baltic's lonely miles. She was nearing her deadweight limit and making a good 17 knots – if anything, with her propellers sunk deeper beneath the surface there was less underfoot vibration and equally the accommodation block was enjoying a quietness over and above the norm. Discounting any untoward events there was every chance that she would put more than 400 nautical miles behind her in the course of the next 24 hours.

Conditions were good. At long last we had shaken off the dreaded sea mist that had inhabited the northern Baltic for the past three days. Today it was a deep blue Baltic, a sea that stretched to a hard unbroken line that ringed 360 degrees around us. It was a sea bearing no spite or vengeance; to a set pattern of its oncoming corrugations we rolled gently at an agreeable frequency.

Mid-morning arrived and we levelled with the Market Lighthouse. At that stage we had completed the last limb of a 100-mile 'dog leg' around the Åland Island group. Third Officer Willie Maclaughlan, alone and master of all before him, reset the autopilot. In response the ship's head smoothly crept round to starboard until it settled on 208 degrees. There it was locked and there it would stay for the next 300 miles.

This was a day when both ship and crew could go about their work without the pressures of port. On these occasions three or four able seamen would spend much of the working day with paint brushes in their hands. Bulwarks, rails, superstructure and decks – every square inch of the mass of external steelwork needed a periodic coat of paint. *Enterprise* was no longer a new ship; the elements were her enemies. Year round exposure to wind and rain, ice, salt, frost and grime took its toll – it was the Chief Officer's responsibility to arrange a schedule that systematically brought the ship back to her former glory.

In following this programme, the Bo'sun would gather his men at the paint store and issue out gallons of white, green or maybe grey. From there they would set off to whichever was the lee side of the ship and set to work with either roller or brush. The external surface of the hull was of course a separate entity and, when at sea, unavailable for painting. This was a job that had to be carried out whilst the ship was docked. Then one would see the seamen at the quayside occupied with long-handled brushes or rollers coating grey paint over the rubs and grazes that inevitably accumulate through repetitive berthing or scrubbing against lock walls.

That Thursday morning a fresh green carpet of paint was being laid on the port side of the main deck. Simultaneously, in more artistic vein, Bo'sun Edwards worked from scaffolding that had been erected alongside the funnel housing. There, in red, buff and white, he freshened up the large U.B.C. anchor and chain house logo emblem that embellished the upper superstructure.

It was the main deck 'wet paint' barrier that halted my morning ramble at the open galley door. Through that portal, zealously employed in overbearing heat, were Head Cook John Jubb and Second Cook Richard Oakley. 'Chef's special' on the lunch menu was to be grilled pork chop, apple sauce, potatoes, sprouts etc. Along with the entrée, cold table and dessert, the main course preparation was in its final throes. Though the hands on the wall clock crept close to lunch hour the two white-garbed cooks moved between the large centre island stove, worktops and cupboards with unrushed control.

John Jubb had been head cook aboard the *Baltic Enterprise* since her maiden voyage. He was a lean six foot plus, with a fresh complexion and jovial disposition. His bright personality matched the quality of his cuisine – without question he was well liked throughout the ship.

"It pays not to cross the cook!" was his flippant reply when earlier I had challenged him with this statement. In all frankness John Jubb openly believed that a well fed crew is a happy crew. In adhering to this principal he had earned great esteem among the fraternity with whom he sailed.

The well equipped galley was situated on the Main Deck.

Richard Oakley was a fellow who backed Jubb in a certain unpretentious manner. Doctrined by the noise, heat, pressure and often angular difficulties of the work in a 'moving' kitchen, Oakley would voice his opinions accordingly. Being Jubb's understudy, Oakley was promoted to head cook whenever leave commitments demanded this. During the period when either of the men was ashore a third member of the team (assistant cook) filled the gap. On this voyage it was his turn to be absent.

Lacking nothing by way of the latest domestic gadgetry, the face of the galley was that of any modern catering unit. Its spaciousness led one to believe that it had the capacity to cater for a number of people far greater than the thirty-one then onboard. Naturally there was a strong emphasis on cleanliness and hygiene; here I felt that the *Enterprise* galley would supersede standards expected in shore catering.

My visits to the galley were never prolonged. It was an area where the intensive efforts of those employed within left a slothful passenger feeling somewhat guilty. Equally, being a place of hotplates and ovens, mincers and mixers, knives and butcher's blocks that could pitch or roll at the whim of the ocean, it held latent perils for the unaccustomed.

Unless one moved fluidly around the ship it would have appeared unlikely that she was carrying a crew of twenty-six. But twenty-six there most definitely were. These men had a rigid pattern of commitments that spread them diversely between galley and radio room, deck and accommodation area, and bridge and engine room. The often empty decks, lounges and alleyways laid emphasis on these work arrangements. Also contributing to the scarcity of stairway traffic was the upstairs-downstairs situation that segregated officers and ratings. Totalling fifteen men, those who inhabited the lower accommodation were socially apart from the rest of the ship. Away from their work, stewards, cooks and seamen were never seen above main deck level. Theirs was a separate world to which, after the arena of watch-keeping, dish washing or stewarding, they returned.

The seamen's accommodation area was a region that had always escaped the infiltration of passengers and was likely to remain so. In this respect, as a passenger occupying some of the grandest quarters aboard, dining with the senior officers and making note of all before me, it was naturally not easy to become accepted when invading this stronghold. Individually, I had arrived on equal terms with the more senior men there. But collectively, looked upon as an alien from above, my presence there was regarded with an element of suspicion. This in no way relegated my admiration for the role that the seamen played; I was more than conscious of the fact that without their labours the ship would never put to sea.

There was no wastage of labour. To keep the ship on an incessant course of freight ferrying the presence of each and every man was essential; in context it was a team in which all from master to pantry boy played a vital role. Though the traditional divisions of rank were in full effect, there was no apparent undertow of disapproval. All knew it was the occupational responsibility attached to a crewman's work that bonded his place in the team.

During the course of that Thursday afternoon I was to see for the first time a full assembly of the crew. In this I was to witness an occasion where officers and men were side by side physically involved in a common cause.

*

While at sea there was the odd occasion when one was startled by the fixed clamour of an emergency alarm system. More often than not this was identified as something of little significance and within minutes silence reigned along the rooms and alleyways once more. However, in mid-Baltic, with no sight of any other shipping, no sign of land and *Baltic Enterprise* cleaving an arrow-straight course across the deep blue water, one would not have predicted any immediate change. Yet the peace that surrounded that afternoon was to be irreparably broken by the fearsome belling of the alarm. This was not the usual evocative warning – it had been preceded by seven short blasts!

I was one of several who, reacting to the alarm, emerged from their quarters donning a bulky, bright orange lifejacket. At the after rail I was ushered to the boat deck where on the starboard side a mixed group of crewmen were rapidly uncovering a white and orange hulled lifeboat. Having been reduced to 'slow ahead' *Enterprise* wallowed aimlessly at the will of a lethargic Baltic tempo. A gathering of some twenty plus life-jacketed people stood back as Peter Green took charge of the situation. On his commands a carefully drilled team lowered the davit arms from which the boat was suspended. Two decks above, pacing the bridge wing, Gerry Brazendale was seen to look at his wristwatch. He was there alone; all of his three deck officers were now involved in the boat launching.

As the lifeboat levelled with the green deck and overhung deep water, Bernard Elworthy and an able seaman urgently scrambled aboard. There was room enough for thirty-eight people aboard but today its role was to carry but two men. Several moments passed as adjustments were made to the davits and release lines and then all heads craned over the rails as the three-ton lifeboat jerkily made a twenty foot drop towards the sea.

I was simply witnessing an exercise at which regulations demanded the attendance of everyone aboard. At the most appropriate period of the week, the crew practised their lifeboat drill in the form of a mock launching, alternating between the two motorised craft carried aboard. On this occasion the starboard boat's descent was halted before the keel touched the water.

"Unless we drill whilst in dock the boat is not floated," was Green's answer when I queried the 'dry' launching.

Lifeboat drill took place after the ship was slowed mid-Baltic.

Once proved that the launching mechanism was fully serviceable, the sea-skimming lifeboat with its skeletal crew had to be hauled by hand winch back to boat deck level. Greasers and stewards, engineers and cooks, seamen and navigators – paint-stained overalls mixed with navy-blue worsted – as every permutation of crew took turns at cranking the low-geared, two-man apparatus.

When the boat was finally inched back up to its davits, much of the urgency had dissipated. Light-hearted ridicule was flung around as breathless personnel discarded their restrictive lifejackets and flopped against the rails. Cigarettes were lit up and the occasion relaxed into an unpremeditated outdoor social gathering.

Why on such an advanced vessel was there no powered recovery system for the lifeboat? It had long been secured inboard and the ship returned to its normal gait when, whilst on the bridge, I questioned Peter Green about the afternoon's event.

"I suppose lifeboats are only intended to go in one direction – it is getting them away safely that counts. Here it must be totally independent of all the ship's power systems; so recovery is an equally 'powerless' operation."

While I accompanied the Chief Officer on watch that evening he remarked that we were exactly six days and one thousand, nine hundred miles out of Hull and now scheduled to be berthed at Purfleet for early Sunday morning. For the moment however, three miles over to port, the long profile of Gotland provided a continuous source of interest. We had been cruising in company with this large island's western seaboard since late afternoon.

Gotland is eighty miles in length and over thirty miles wide, it is the most easterly province of Sweden but in character remains a separate entity. Stemming back thousands of years, its illustrious history would fill many chapters. During the Middle Ages it was the greatest trading place in Northern Europe. Visby, its capital, was accepted as one of the major cities in the world. Largely controlled by German merchants, the community gained wealth comparable to that of London or Paris. At one stage in history Visby became the battleground of various Baltic powers. Consequently Gotland changed hands many times until, in 1645, it finally became sealed to the Swedish nation.

Visby lies mid way along Gotland's 80-mile western seaboard.

Modern day Gotland enjoys a flourishing tourist industry. Its extensive coastline embraces thirty sandy beaches, some are remote quiet coves backed by dark green pine forests, and others have camping sites that reach down to the water's edge. But the main attraction is Visby itself. Ranking among the most interesting and well preserved medieval cities in Europe, it is a place of many traditional and cultural attractions. The fairytale city walls still display an almost unbroken fortification two miles in length and sport thirty-seven towers.

From the decks of our ship, Visby slowly unveiled its medieval charm. Lit up by the evening sun was a vista of tall, red-roofed houses, embattled walls and, above all, the three domed towers of its majestic cathedral. Fronting all this was a picturesque harbour thronged with all manner of colourful craft.

Through the glasses Gotland provided a compelling scene that steadily changed as *Enterprise* continued to plough southwards. Church spires and windmill towers broke the flat masses of skyline forests while at the foreshore undercut craggy cliffs gave way to tree-fringed coves and sandy beaches. By co-ordinating information from the chart table at the latter stages of our Gotland sail-past, Peter Green and I were able to pick out the rocky islets of Lilla Karlsö and Stora Karlsö. Apart from seeing the breeding grounds for huge colonies of seabirds, visitors there are likely to discover many uncommon plants wedged among the rocky outcrops.

As we pushed on towards the night Gotland reluctantly slipped beyond the darkening horizon – we were once more alone in a spacious sea lane.

During my voyage aboard the *Baltic Enterprise* I was regularly served reminders of the severe winter conditions Baltic shipping has to face. In January and February ice usually grips the Baltic Sea as far south as Gotland. Sometimes, in the hardest of winters, the sea can freeze over as far as the reaches of Copenhagen or Kiel Bay. I had listened to a whole string of stories covering the trauma of shipping in the battle for survival against ice conditions; such as the time when the Finnish icebreaker *Varma* rescued the *Baltic Jet* from the brink of being bowled over by an ever advancing wall of pressure ice several miles south of Helsinki. Or the occasion when, having been in collision with the powerful breaker *Tarmo*, the entire crew of the badly damaged *Baltic Sprite* narrowly escaped being stranded for the winter at Finland's northernmost port of Kemi.

There was talk of pilots skiing or motoring over the ice in order to reach incoming vessels – of crewmen walking across a deserted wilderness from a stranded ship to the shore – of times when having struggled for days to reach the Finnish coast, stores were exchanged between neighbouring icebound vessels by use of sledges – and when fresh water systems had gone solid and the accommodation blackened by rimed windows and port holes.

Most of the dialogue was issued from the etched memories of the crew's more senior citizens, for in the main the tales dated back to the 50s and 60s when U.B.C. had a considerable fleet of small conventional freighters. Representing the younger blood aboard Bernard Elworthy, Paul Davey and George Hall were restricted to the 70s when the advent of the larger ro-ro ships and the introduction of more effective icebreakers had lessened the degree of combat against the northern winters.

Baltic Enterprise **was locked in Baltic pressure ice 40 miles south of Helsinki during the winter of 1977.** (Photo by Chief Officer Peter Green.)

Not as if the elements were any more benevolent towards modern ships. Like against like, both types of vessels had faced the same cruel conditions. Yet, where the soaring high sides of a ro-ro ship lift the crew and their accommodation way above and out of contact with the frozen surface, those travelling aboard a deeply laden conventional freighter are sat low and physically surrounded by jagged floes that have been thrust upwards by the ship's forward progress. When in this situation the visual aspect alone falls nothing short of dramatic.

To round off a lengthy bout of 'ice talk' on that seventh night at sea, John Gunning delivered more photographic evidence of the Baltic's potentially unyielding winter grip. The few who drifted from the smoke room's comfortable armchairs to the Second Engineer's cabin saw, projected onto a white sheeted bulkhead, colour slides taken aboard *Baltic Enterprise* herself the previous winter. Though the ship had a fully ice-strengthened hull and theoretically the potential of breaking through a crust of up to one metre thick, the pictures revealed her uncompromisingly blocked within a vast frozen arena.

Stage by stage the slides illustrated how on her way north, *Enterprise* had scraped, smashed, jolted and eventually stopped in the most solid ice mass encountered in her Baltic ferrying history.

"At first the sensation was that of running into a crusty reef that gave way to our seemingly remorseless momentum. Then as the ice thickened and closed in, one noticed marked changes in the ship's attitude. Unfamiliar sounds became considerably louder and more frequent; at the same time her progress became more hindered and fell into an irregular pattern. Over the side, twenty feet below the weather deck, the massive ice slabs being lifted by the bow progressively dropped back on themselves and crashed in rugged peaks against the ship's hull. With attendant jolting the noises took on a melée of scraping, crashing and hollow banging that one would expect to hear if the ship were being driven across a boulder strewn bottom. Sometimes the ship would be drawn to a halt. Here it was necessary to backtrack down our own self-carved channel then charge at a full 'ten ahead' to meet the ice with all available force."

John Gunning's commentary was in sequence with a series of transparencies that had been taken from the upper decks of the ship. "Eventually we arrived at a situation where the buckled ice surface began to close in behind us. Soon this was to end the ramming technique so, despite all efforts we became icebound forty miles or so short of Helsinki."

Enterprise was not alone in this predicament for in the winter sunlight the camera had picked out a varied assortment of shipping littering the ice at all angles over an area covering several square miles. Even after being released by one of the efficient Finnish icebreakers the ro-ro's problems were not concluded – her generous 73-foot beam proved to be an encumbrance in the narrow closing channel carved by the rescue breaker, and further bouts of strenuous bludgeoning were needed before she reached port.

There were also shots taken during the same term of events of a rescued coaster with its bows lashed to the stern of the attendant icebreaker. Sailing in tandem, the coaster's own engine was adding to the breaker's cause.

The picture show highlighted a contrasting perspective of the Baltic to the one which the ongoing voyage had revealed. Yet it held a compelling impact – one to which I responded by vowing to return one future winter and sample myself.

After punching through a northerly Baltic gale one winter night the deck crew braved to venture to the foredeck where they found that the continuous bludgeoning of big seas had left sea spray that had frozen on every inch of steel. In places the rime was almost one foot thick. It was estimated that overall the ship was carrying four hundred tons of Baltic Sea ice. Pictured are the initial efforts to clear the mooring windlass and doorway – the rails above remaining frozen solid.

12. Kiel Canal Passage

When choosing a course on which to sail between the Baltic and North Seas, a sea captain has three principal options. In brief these are namely the 'Great Belt', the 'Sound' and the Kiel Canal.

In deciding which route to take, he has to take into consideration the size of his ship, weather conditions, his time schedule and the fuel and pilotage costs to the owners. For those in command of the largest ships that ply between these two seas, the 'Great Belt' is the only option available. When leaving the Baltic on this passage, he steers his ship between the Danish islands of Fyn and Zealand, then continues north through the Kattegat to Skagen and The Skaw. In distance this is the longest of the three routes but its straits provide the deepest and widest channel. Of the 'Sound,' the crossing we have already covered, it should be mentioned that, being limited to carrying ships of no more than 7.5 metres draught, it is the most restrictive of the three routes.

Thirdly, the Kiel Canal is the most favoured route for sea traffic movements between the Baltic ports and those to the southern North Sea – and onwards. Effectively the canal clips approximately 250 nautical miles off such a voyage so, when considering ever increasing fuel costs, it presents an attractive proposition. However, on face value the saving in passage time is nothing like so great. Shipping using the 60-mile canal is restricted to a maximum speed of eight knots; thus it takes between seven and eight hours to complete the average passage. Compared to a fair-weather passage around The Skaw the saving in time can be as little as two hours. However, when gales rage across the waters of northern Denmark, which in winter they often do, the savings in time and fuel make the Kiel Canal appealing from every angle.

Though we had been enjoying fair weather on our homeward voyage through the Baltic, Gerry Brazendale had elected to travel the Kiel Canal to effect the shortest passage to the Thames. This was in no way an unusual decision for, though as master he had the authority to choose the course his ship would take, it was regular practice for ships on the Finanglia operation both inward and outward of the Purfleet base to use the canal.

Geographically the Kiel Canal lies within the boundaries of West Germany. It severs the low-lying neck of land that ultimately supports the Danish mainland – known as Jutland. The waterway follows a wavering course in a general N.E./S.W. direction. Specifically it links the south-west corner of the Baltic at Kiel Bay with the River Elbe downstream from Hamburg, twenty-five miles from the North Sea. From a passenger's point of view the Kiel passage was an added bonus to the Scandinavian voyage. Breaking halfway across the homeward leg it came as a timely relief to a three-day seascape.

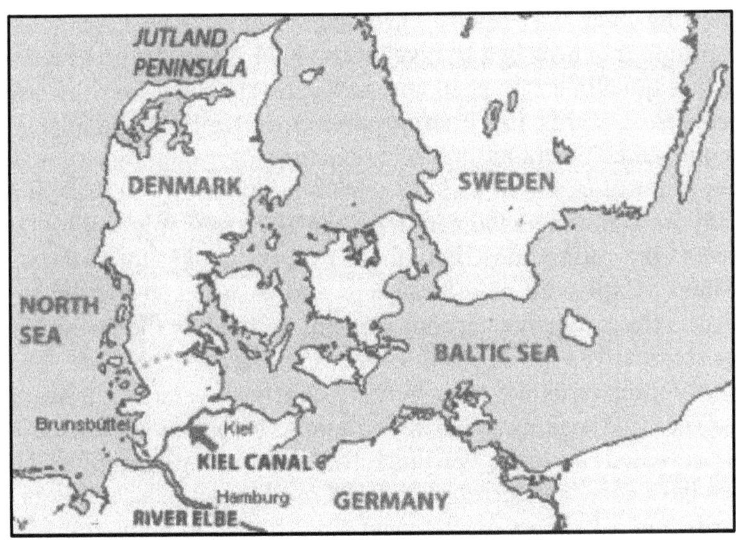

An average of 250 miles are saved by using the 60-mile Kiel Canal as an alternative to sailing around the Jutland Peninsula.

Having progressively hauled southwards overnight, we had passed the Olands Sodra Grund Lighthouse (known as 'Old Sod' to our navigators) and then briefly backtracked our outward course between the Swedish mainland and Bornholm Island. From then onwards, throughout Friday morning, *Enterprise* had been held on a south-westerly heading making for the extremities of the southern Baltic.

Though the sea state had been slight, offering our ship a smooth carefree run, it had become increasingly more populated. None the least significant among the miscellany of ships we met or joined forces with along the latter stage of our Baltic voyage was a flotilla of West German naval gunboats. Numbering eight in all these identical craft sped close by our port side heading, in arrow straight line astern, purposely towards the open sea. At the time our ship was being navigated along a closely buoyed channel that carried us almost westwards through the Fehmarn Belt. To the north these straits were fringed by the shores of the Danish island of Lolland while to the south and beyond our port side rail lay Puttgarden – a village on the German Fehmarn Island and a strategic point of the Belt ferry link.

Two hours later, thirty-five miles on and approaching mid-afternoon, our unerring pace was briefly curtailed when, at Kiel Lighthouse, we were brought to a near halt to take on the Kiel Pilot. His presence on the bridge was quickly established and under his guidance we soon resumed our progress towards the inviting stretch of Kiel Bay (Kieler Förde) which presented itself as a bright expanse of water punctuated with clusters of multi-coloured sailed yachts and dinghies. The very fact that Kiel Bay was chosen as the venue for the 1972 Olympic sailing regattas illustrates the attraction that these waters hold for international yachtsmen. A splendid new 800-berth marina was constructed to stage the event – this exclusive harbour was pin-pointed by the forest of masts over to starboard as our ship slid further into the bay.

Shortly afterwards we were in more confined waters on a heading of 195 degrees and making a sedate ten knots. Now, having closed in, the shores revealed a scene varying from charming sea-edge holiday villages backed by soft green woodland on the east bank to unobtrusive shipyards and a heliport on the west side. It was in company with that more commercialised west shore that the deepwater channel led us. It not only served the canal with a continuous stream of traffic, it was also the main arterial route to the bustling port of Kiel.

Kiel itself is a city of 250,000 inhabitants and capital of the state of Schleswig-Holstein. It straggles abundantly around the head of the tideless, twelve-mile 'Förde' displaying a pulsating activism. Capitalising on its natural harbour location, Kiel has developed to become one of Germany's main industrial centres. As a port it facilitates every type of freight and is the terminal for numerous ferry services.

But the thrusting centre of Kiel was not for us. Halfway along the shore that would have carried us there the Pilot had the ship brought to a near halt. We had arrived at Holtenau, the starting place for our canal journey. For a while *Enterprise* ambled on sunlit water in an undecided manner – likewise did the small coaster that had followed us a cable distance astern on our passage across the bay. Our wait was simply an execution of the Highway Code – there were traffic lights on the shore that clearly indicated that we were not to proceed. They favoured a variegated string of commercial shipping that was soon to emerge from the canal channel. For a time the scene was that of a High Street junction, for astern of us two more vessels had joined the queue. The marshalling was conducted under strict control and with the passing of the last of the largest vessels we were allowed to proceed.

The odd assortment of ships that were now heading seawards down the bay had been released from one of the huge locks that straddled across the canal entrance – this particular lock pit was now vacant and offering us an open invitation.

"Hard to starboard!" was the command from the Pilot directing operations within the bridgehouse.

Approached from Kiel Bay, Holtenau is the eastern gateway to the canal. Our canal transit commenced passing through the same lock as the ship photographed here.

Out at the port wing control position Gerry Brazendale was at the ready – it would be he who would present *Enterprise* to the lock.

Holtenau had two pairs of locks – large and small, respectively new and old. We were destined for the 'north' pit of the larger pair. Being over 1,000 feet in length and almost 150 feet in breadth each of these 'large' locks would theoretically accommodate four ships of *Enterprise*'s dimensions. Being free to enter an empty pit of such proportions Brazendale was able to manoeuvre the ship with ease – unlike the tight lock situation that I had witnessed at Hull a week earlier. Subsequently we were quickly moored in the lock with our port side at the centre island quay.

Although the origins of the Kiel Canal date back to the early 19th century when the territory belonged to the Danes, the waterway that exists today was a product of German ingenuity during the period between 1888 and 1895. Officially opened on January 21st, 1895, by Emperor Wilhelm II, it was duly named the Kaiser-Wilhelm Canal. It was soon an established route highly beneficial to the exchange of goods between nations along the Baltic coasts and their worldwide trade partners. Such was the impact of the new North Sea/Baltic route that as early as 1899 it enjoyed an annual traffic flow of 26,000 ships. Realising the strategic importance of the canal the Germans were quick to extend its potential. Between 1904 and 1914 it was both deepened and widened; thus it was capable of carrying the large warships that they were energetically building prior to World War I.

The Kiel Canal (known in Germany as the Nord-Ostsee-Kanal) is open to shipping day and night throughout the year. Being the most used sea-linking canal in the world it is estimated that on a yearly average one vessel passes through every eight minutes. Charges for ships (canal dues, pilotage fees etc.) are based on gross tonnage. Due to the ever continuing rise of fuel prices ship owners find the canal an effective means of containing overheads.

We shared the lock with four other craft – two coasters of around 500 gross tons, a Polish freighter of similar size to ourselves (which to my amazement had such a surplus of crew that no fewer than fourteen men attended the forward mooring deck) and finally a thirty-foot cruiser yacht that had gingerly entered the lock pit when all the 'hardware' had been securely moored. In close company with towering commercial ships, its white fibreglass hull looked as vulnerable as an egg in a box of sledgehammers.

Once the seaward gates had closed and the lock began to fill, our short break at Holtenau was almost at an end. At the quayside was a small shop and post office. It was there especially for the convenience of seamen from ships passing through the locks. I watched three of our crewmen dash from its doors and along the scrupulously tidy precincts to the rising bulk of the ship where their companions were continually adjusting the accommodation ladder to the new level. Slow service was one commodity the shop could not afford to put on offer!

Having locks on either side, the Kiel-Holtenau Harbour Master's Office was effectually on an island noteworthy for its scrupulously landscaped grounds.

When level with the expanse of canal water that had magically opened up, *Enterprise* had regained her true height. From the 'monkey island' Bob and Ruth Turnbull and I took in an observation platform vista much dissimilar to the deep-blue circle of the ocean. Holtenau appeared as a most pleasant residential suburb of Kiel. Amid the lush green cover of the northern bank's broad-leafed trees were many avenues of fine houses. It was a place that spelled prosperity – not the least in the tidy commercial premises that lined the canal's southern shore. These were chiefly bases of the internationally known oil companies. At their quays ships could conveniently berth and re-bunker before heading back to sea. At the lock side were railed promenades from which the general public could while away an hour or so watching the ships go by. The immediate area was neatly lawned and gardened. In particular I noted the harbourmaster's offices directly on the lock gates; set within its grassed frontage was a landscaped mosaic of the West German national emblem. In similar vein on the opposite shore the U.B.C. offices (the company had acted as agents for shipping using the canal since 1946) were fronted by a wide patio that also overlooked the canal's endless activity.

Underway, at a most dignified pace, we were soon to pass beneath two closely linked, high-level road bridges. They were the first of seven imposing bridge structures that at various stages carry both road and rail over the sixty mile waterway. The minimum height of these bridges over the waterway is 137 feet – the maximum height allowed for masts of ships being 132 feet.

Onwards from the Holtenau bridges we cruised slowly into the heart of the German countryside. If not spectacular the scenery held a strange fascination – the unlikely event of a large sea-going vessel journeying between green fields where cattle grazed, wooded hillsides in which rabbits scurried and parklands where families picnicked had suddenly moved into reality. All credit to the German authorities for making an amenity of the canal side. Down its cobbled banks young and old sat fishing, others strolled along miles of well-surfaced towpaths or were there just to feed the ducks and swans that bobbed on the gently rolling wake of passing ships. Inns and restaurants boasted gardens or patios that reached down to the water's edge. Car parks were at regular intervals, sometimes in woodland clearings that offered an unhindered view of the passing scene. Along the route people often gave a friendly wave, a greeting to which the small group on *Enterprise's* high decks cheerfully responded.

At Holtenau the canal's broad waterway spreads between a smart residential suburb of Kiel and ships' quayside refuelling facilities.

The Levensaur High Bridge was built in 1893 to carry both rail and road traffic.

Always there were ships. Astern, those that had shared the lock kept a respectable distance. From ahead came a regular flow of assorted tonnage. Mostly they were smaller vessels than our own – tugs, barges, naval craft and pleasure boats – more common than any were deep-laden coasters inevitably registered at Hamburg or Antwerp. One of

151

these hardworking vessels still bore scars of the long past winter in as much as the lower half of her hull was completely stripped of paint.

"Ice scrubbed," an equally astonished Peter Green called up from the port wing.

Infrequently we met up with larger ships. On these occasions great caution was exercised. Large ships moving in close company are known to attract each other like magnets. Likewise two vessels with a big displacement passing in a confined channel can create a massive tidal surge – one which could seriously erode the canal's banks. To eliminate such happenings, passing places were provided at eleven selected points along the route. In conjunction there was a tightly controlled signalling system, directions from which all craft must conform to.

On the Kiel transit we passed under seven high level bridges and near to many fine country houses. The ship's 'Monkey Island' providing a splendid viewing platform.

Having travelled at the regulation 8 knot maximum for more than two hours (often in company with horse riders, joggers or cyclists) we were confronted by high-pyloned traffic lights that flashed continually at red. Our canal pilot had *Enterprise* brought into a starboard side lay-by at that point and held hard against the high dolphins there. *Antoni*

Granuszewski was the name spread across the Polish-registered freighter that had eventually rounded a distant tree-shaded bend. Though of considerable tonnage the vessel would fall well short of the 771 feet length and 106 feet breadth maximum permissible size to transit the canal.

"It's like dining on a slow-moving railcar," our young American travelling companions commented as, from the dinner table, we looked out over a steadily changing rural scene.

How right they were; had we been seated in the dining car of a German train the general aspect of the neighbouring farmsteads, thatched cottages and individually designed houses would have been no different. But the novelty of sailing overland meant nothing to our mariner hosts. They had voyaged the Kiel many times; to them the green fields through the port side windows were just pictures on the walls. Inevitably their line of conversation would revert to the turnround at Purfleet, the port engine gear case, the latest cricket scores or the weather.

In this respect Brazendale and Green had shared the dinner hour between the bridge and the table. They had brought with them news of impending bad weather. Away from the two spells of fog and rain met around the Finnish coast we had, over the past week, become somewhat complacent about climatic conditions. Now, with a depression rapidly approaching the 'high' over northern Europe, a gale warning had been issued for most U.K. sea areas – German Bight, Humber and Thames included. From this forecast there was a strong possibility that, at the 'eleventh hour' of the voyage, we would be met with south-westerly winds of force eight or nine.

"Should nicely meet it in the Elbe estuary." Having read the Radio Officer's report Brazendale blandly explained his calculations to his five enquiring passengers. "Summer gales are far from unknown in the North Sea but, if it's any consolation, unlike winter storms, they seldom last. From November onwards north-easterlies can blow with no respite for more than a week on end. Sometimes we have weathered them across to Skagen or Kiel on our outward route to Finland, had a comparatively smooth Baltic passage but then re-engaged the very same North Sea gale on the homeward leg."

Approaching the halfway stage of our Kiel Canal journey, we passed through Rendsburg. With 50,000 inhabitants this was the only place of substance encountered between the terminals of the canal. Though essentially an inland town, Rendsburg capitalises on its waterside location – from the decks of our ship, shipbuilding was an industry much in evidence. In this direction I was informed that it was at these yards that many of U.B.C.'s past conventional freighters had been built.

Nearer the town we looked down on quays and wharfs at which coasters, petroleum carriers and freighters (that I guessed were carrying grain) were moored. We travelled through built-up areas where attractive steep-roofed houses with observation patios overlooked the water, where roadways carried cars and lorries close and parallel with the ship. There were areas where tree-fringed promenades gave residents the opportunity to closely view the canal's endless flow of maritime traffic. Through the large picture windows of a modern-styled waterfront hotel diners looked out as our ship passed by. Simultaneously there were guests watching from bedroom balconies; seemingly, had we been a little closer, we could have reached out to shake them by the hand.

Adding to the interest generated by Rendsburg's waterside buildings were the various ingenious means of linking the two shores thereabouts. First there had been high-speed traffic flying over our heads on a leggy concrete bridge carrying the Hamburg/Flensburg autobahn. Its angular main span had taken one straight and slender leap directly over the shimmering waterway. Within a mile was one of the twelve selected points where small ferries carried cars and passengers free of charge to and fro between either bank.

Close to the hub of Rendsburg was a most unusual steel railway viaduct. To gain sufficient height to cross the canal, it spiralled through a complete 360 degrees. This massive loop, somewhere in the order of one mile in diameter and gradually rising above the town, looked as though it belonged to an oversized funfair. Not only did it whisk Kiel-bound trains high over the canal but it also carried road vehicles at a lower level. Suspended beneath the main span was a moving platform that travelled smoothly between the two banks several feet above the water. Obviously, having to cross such a busy waterway on a regular basis, the transporter's brief journey had to be carefully timed. I noticed that while *Enterprise* was beneath the bridge and directly abeam of the platform it had already commenced its 550-foot trek. By the time our ship had cleared the bridge, the transporter, with a load of ten cars, was directly astern and halfway across the canal. Soon the ship trailing our wake was level with the bridge, by then the suspended platform had reached its destination – split second timing!

Shortly after a ship has passed under the Rendsburg High Bridge its ten-car capacity 'transporter' platform wastes no time in making the 550-foot canal crossing.

Finally, past the south-western boundary of Rendsburg, a deep gorge had been carved out of the landscape at either side and at right angles to the canal. Within the cleft of this disturbed land ran a broad highway that sped traffic deep beneath our liquid road. The tunnel was a product of the 1960s and carried yet another trunk route between Hamburg and Denmark.

For me, had I not been out on deck at the time, the ship's brief halt at a point west of Rendsburg would have gone unnoticed. We had arrived at the canal's mid-distance mark and here abeam to starboard was the main pilot exchange station – a building that resembled one of the more modern and sophisticated railway signal boxes.

Since Holtenau we had been navigated by a dedicated canal pilot who had brought his own helmsman aboard. This was no disrespect aimed at the ability of *Enterprise's* own deck crew – canal regulations demand that ships of a certain size engage both pilot and helmsmen for the journey. Needless to say this was not a complete takeover. Our watch-keeping officer was on the bridge at all times and whenever there was any close manoeuvring to be carried out Gerry Brazendale appeared from the shadows. At this halfway point, the Holtenau pilot left the ship to be replaced by a further pilot who would guide us to Brunsbüttel on the northern bank of the River Elbe.

A fussing pilot boat was quickly discarded from our ship's towering side and again we progressed serenely across the northern neck of West Germany. On this leg it appeared that the further we travelled the more flat and monotonous the countryside became. But by now the day was ageing, and gathering clouds brought a premature darkness over the scene – navigation lights glowing, we moved on towards the night.

Indoors the quiet of the boat deck level had been lifted through an unusually well attended social hour in the smoke room. Several of the younger officers had taken a communal sauna and their ignited faces warmed the bar-side scene. There was little doubt that the congenial mood had been raised through a configuration of circumstances: the relaxed pace of the ship; the seemingly appropriate tunes from Carl's guitar; and for some the prospect of taking leave on arrival in the U.K.

I too began to think of our landfall but not specifically in a euphoric way. Unlike the crewmen I was on leave, a leave that was now drawing nearer to an end with every mile the ship sailed. Saturday was but an hour away; in a little more than two days' time I would again be lingering at the sea shore en route for work. All too soon I would have to step away from this world of incessant ferrying; such a time when I would turn my back on this ship and her crew. Yet I had a mandate to transcribe the experience of travelling aboard the *Baltic Enterprise* for the enlightenment and hopefully the enjoyment of others; therefore I would not be completely severed from her.

Thirty minutes past midnight and our Kiel Canal journey was over. Brunsbüttel's outer lock gates had retracted to release *Baltic Enterprise* onto an inky black channel that curved gently away to starboard. Overhead, solid cloud cover blanketed out the night sky – it was dark and, moreover, there was a hint of rain in the gathering wind that plucked at my clothes. On rounding the beacons that marked the outer limit of the channel we laboriously started to roll. This was the River

Elbe – at that point over one mile wide and twenty-five miles from the sea.

The lights of Brunsbüttel had glowed abundantly, radiating a scene far remote from that described by John Garvey, when as a lad he had first sailed to the town. "World War II had just ended and the people here were on the verge of starvation. It was a pathetic sight – they came down to the ships carrying their last possessions to barter or simply beg for food."

But today's affluent Brunsbüttel was dropping astern and now, in response to the pilot's calculated orders, our ship had been steered to the buoyed channel that pointed us seaward. Once more the engines had broken into full cry and the ship's inevitable mood of urgency had been restored. Gale warning apart we had embarked on a 400-mile haul across a stretch of unpredictable water.

Before turning in, I tugged up my collar and took a lonely walk on the windswept deck. As I watched, the shore illuminations settled into the distance; a curtain had been drawn across the canal and a sixty mile passage that had added a further dimension to my voyage.

The western entrance to the canal is approached from the River Elbe at Brundsbüttel.

13. The Inhospitable North Sea

Daybreak, a reluctant late summer daybreak, with a spume-streaked sea that boiled incessantly into the hazy-grey horizon. The rain-laden, south-westerly wind impelled an endless succession of white-capped waves into walls of fury. Amid this turbulent sea the *Baltic Enterprise* pitched and rolled in a continuous sequence of submission. Such was the geometry of the sea's surface that I likened it to a vast estate of steep-roofed houses – and in this context we plunged from roof tops to gardens in sickening falls that left the stomach churning twenty feet above.

With each successive surge our burdened ro-ro ship buried her bow deep into the base of the salt-sea furrow. Then while still shuddering through the impact, she laboriously elevated her bulwarks through the maelstrom of white water until they angled to the grey-lined sky. Simultaneously her stern settled into the trough with quavering proclamation of burrowing screws. Being driven at near maximum power and being held tight on course by her autopilot *Enterprise* was obliged to progress directly into the gale. This blatant attack upon the elements induced violent eruptions of crippled water to spray high over and across the container-laden weather deck. Together with wind-driven rain, a desultory fog of sea spray partially shrouded the superstructure tower. The prospect through the salt-rimed bridgehouse windows was one of a climatic revolt.

Sleep had not been forthcoming. The ever increasing movement of the ship was gradually spreading each and every loose item across the cabin carpet. My 'pad' had become alive with unfamiliar sounds. Creaks and groans were cast from wardrobe doors and deck-head panel seams, window blinds snapped continually against the glass and my dressing gown swished through an ever widening arc on its bulkhead peg. Before the cabin was reduced to a state of turmoil I had rolled from beneath the duvet and unsteadily stowed my things.

This was no longer the luxuriously secure world to which I had blamelessly become accustomed. With top clothes over my nightwear I swayed across the brightly lit alleyway towards the stairway to the bridge. I was not alone. Awake for his early engine room watch John Gunning had also adopted the same inquisitive state of mind. Together we discreetly entered the swaying bridgehouse.

Moving around in the half light were three navigators. Bernard Elworthy, whose watch had fifteen minutes to run, Peter Green ready to take on his early stint and the Master, who had hardly left the bridge since Brunsbüttel.

According to the chart that Elworthy was busily pencilling up to date, the last three hours had yielded no more than forty miles. Having passed the German fishing town of Cuxhaven to port one hour earlier, we had now put twelve miles between our rolling stern and the Elbe estuary. Thirty miles to the south the coastline contour swept down to Bremerhaven and the River Weser, northwards and twenty-five miles away was the tiny island of Heligoland. Our course was 265 degrees. The wind was gusting from ten or more points to port. Gerry Brazendale was monitoring the ship's attitude to the steep seas. Accepting the fact that we were pitching more or less directly into the weather, he knew us to be on a satisfactory course.

The gale appeared as a temporary problem to our mariners. They did not seem to look upon it as a long-term prospect. "Blow itself out by midday," I heard exchanged between them.

Additionally, once further away from the coast they expected the short steep seas to open up. They knew these waters and the influence a westerly gale had upon them. They also knew their ship's capabilities: to the landsman it was being punished, to them *Enterprise* was withstanding yet another spell of bad weather; she had met worse storms, far worse.

Despite their bulk, ro-ro ships are no less vulnerable to severe weather conditions than any other. While wedged in the bridgehouse starboard corner, uncomfortably scribbling my account of the ongoing situation, my thoughts went back to November 1977 and the fate of the 4,500gt Hull-registered *Hero*. Not many miles north-west of our position this ship lay on the seabed of the North Sea under 100 feet of water. At the time of the disaster the *Hero* was operating on her regular service en route from Esbjerg to Grimsby carrying 3,600 tons of unitised freight. Having departed the Danish port in the evening of 11th November the vessel was soon battling with a force eight gale. Just after midnight *Hero* encountered a violent storm with heavy rain, sheet lightning and a wind gusting force ten; she began to ship water.

In common with many ro-ros, *Hero* was a hard pressed ship. The previous year she had been lengthened by the addition of a new 70-foot mid-section. This modification had increased her freight capacity by 40%. Since that time *Hero* had been subjected to a rigorous work schedule through which her managers had requested a three month postponement of her annual survey.

Initially the ingress of seawater was traced to worn rubber seals around ill-fitting stern doors, but soon it was discovered that there were other leaks. Now hove-to and being battered by winds of force eleven, *Hero* took a severe starboard list. In fear of capsize, her Master sent out an S.O.S. which was immediately answered by three vessels in the near vicinity – the motor ship *Valerie,* the Canadian frigate *Huron* and the formidable *Tor Britannia*. Of *Hero's* twenty-seven crew and three passengers, nine were lifted from her upper decks by helicopter to *Tor Britannia,* six were lifted to *Huron* and fourteen in life rafts were taken aboard the *Valerie.* One crew member died having suffered a heart attack while climbing a ship-side ladder. The *Hero* sank by the stern some twenty-eight hours after being abandoned.

A pre-lengthening photo of Ellerman's Wilson Line 4,500gt. ro-ro freighter *Hero* which was lost off Heligoland during the North Sea storm 13th November 1977.

At breakfast time and four hours on we were punching a course of 252 degrees. This carried us directly into the wind and parallel with the Frisian Island chain. Respectively, from east to west, this string of twenty or so islands came under the German and Dutch flags.

With the day now fully awake, the prospect through the salt-sprayed windows appeared less hostile than at dawn. The rain had ceased and a smattering of sunlit patches appeared amid the windswept clouds. Above and beyond the spray shroud that periodically fused from festoons of bow-smashed water, the sea surface showed an oscillating circle of blue-grey and white. A more defined wave frequency had been established and now one could begin to predict the ship's motion – yet, despite the brighter outlook, this motion was no less troublesome.

Within the accommodation block familiar surroundings were seen at unfamiliar angles. The imbalance sensation was all consuming – for the first time during the voyage, one had to carefully plan each and every move between strategic points. As the ship plummeted into a trough, the fore-aft alleyways dropped forward to the creaking accompaniment of protesting panel work. While burrowing her bow into an oncoming 'white horse' wave, a mild shudder ran through the length of the hull. Simultaneously the ship's forward progress would be briefly arrested to the extent that one would lurch forward as would a standing passenger on a braking bus. Then as she steadily lifted her head to the wave crest, the carpeted deck would reverse its angle in the fashion of a fun-fair ride – a motion to which the unwary would sway and grasp for support.

Needless to say it was not a situation that stimulated the appetites of non-seafarers. With the absence of three of my fellow passengers, the breakfast table was more forlorn than of late. For a while Bob Turnbull and I sat alone nibbling lightly buttered toast and sipping dark coffee from crockery that clung to a dampened tablecloth. Of the few crew members that popped into the saloon that Saturday morning, Peter Green and John Gunning appeared to be alone in ordering a hearty breakfast. Until their arrival from early watch duties, the menu card had not been considered. On noticing our 'under par' performance at the unlevelling table, they sympathetically advised, "The best way to ward of seasickness is to eat well and keep active."

Bob and I had looked back at the past week and the ongoing gale conditions. "Had we not been diverted to west Finland we would have been alongside at Hull now," Bob had lamented. How right he was. The visit to Turku and Mäntyluoto had been a bonus but now we were paying for it!

By early afternoon *Enterprise* was riding a relentless North Sea swell.

Indeed, the ship was going to arrive back at Hull two days later than originally intended. For my part I had come to terms, that on berthing at Purfleet the following morning, my commitments were such that I had no alternative than to leave the ship and take the train north.

Later, in an effort to 'keep active' I took up a standing invitation to visit the radio room. Considering the normal watch-keeping schedule aboard, Radio Officer Roy Caple had a job apart. Though like any other man aboard he was available for duty throughout the twenty-four hours, his normal working day was split into three periods – 08.00 to 12.00, 15.00 to 17.00 and 20.00 to 22.00. But more significant than his differing work schedule, Roy Caple was the only crew member who was not directly employed by U.B.C. All but the largest U.K. shipping lines contracted their radio officers from specialised radio telegraphy companies. As an employee of Kelvin Hughes, Caple was one from a pool of qualified 'sparks' who were posted to wherever their services were contracted. Likewise was the equipment that he operated – this was installed in the ship by the Kelvin Hughes company on a 'rental' basis.

Roy Caple was a tall, clean-cut young man with a clear determination to succeed in life. In this respect youth was on his side; had we not been carrying a teenage pantry-boy, Caple at twenty-two would have claimed to be the youngest man aboard. Like the Captain he hailed from Dorset. From leaving school he had taken a three year course at Southampton Nautical Collage and qualified as a Radio Officer at the first attempt. After taking a further electronics course, he had secured a job at sea – a career that spanned a modest two years.

He briefly outlined certain aspects of his duties: "Listening out for the ship's call-sign – possibly owners or agents wishing to contact us with orders, traffic lists, weather reports and forecasts, emergency signals and distress calls."

With regard to emergency signals he explained the regulation three-minute silence period 15-18 minutes and 45-48 minutes past every hour. "If a vessel with a low powered transmitter is in difficulties the silence period allows him clear space and a greater opportunity of being heard."

As mentioned earlier, the radio room was located on the port side of the navigating bridge deck directly abaft of the bridgehouse. As the radio officer's living quarters were linked to his place of work, he was the only permanent resident at this deck level. To some degree this arrangement segregated him from the rest of the ship. Away from mealtimes I had seen little of Roy Caple. When our paths had crossed, I found him to be a source of up-to-the-minute information, particularly where the weather was concerned – today was no exception.

"Air pressure is rising again – wind backing southerly – down to force five by mid-afternoon. Should see some sun – get your deck chair booked!"

Though this remark was somewhat presumptuous, the forecast proved to be near accurate. Around 14.30, feeling considerably more attuned to the ship's motion, I ventured out on deck. At first, holding the after rail, I gazed over and afar of our swaying stern. Today the frothing wake that I had often seen linger for miles astern, was quickly spread and dissipated amidst the melée of white-topped waves that challenged *Enterprise*'s progress. Then sneaking gingerly out to the port rail, I was hit by an unyielding wind that seemed determined to take the anorak off my back. The gripping manifestation here was not only the power of the wind as it ripped along the deck, but the noise it created in doing so. Above the roar of the waves that crashed and banged against our lofty steel hull was the scream of the gale as it rushed through the stanchions, halyards and aerials that adorned the upper works.

Improving though they were, conditions did not calm sufficiently to allow one out on deck for any length of time until nightfall. Therefore I utilised much of my time writing up my notes and making the rounds to express my appreciation to the crew for their help and co-operation over the past nine days. Though it was claimed that my inquisitiveness had not been a hindrance I felt that there must have been times when, as a 'fly on the wall', I had been wished well over the horizon!

Such were the last hours and stage of my voyage aboard the *Baltic Enterprise*. With little to see except the lights of the occasional vessel tracing the darkening horizon and, with those aboard tired from the activity of the past twenty-four hours, a subdued mood took away some of the fulfilment of an exceptional vacation. Equally, having myself spent much of the previous night out of bed, I had not escaped tiredness.

14. UK Turnround

Purfleet lies on the north bank of the Thames, approximately halfway between London's Tower Bridge and the river estuary near Southend. Having taken aboard the estuary pilot from a cutter at the Sunk Lightship and exchanged him for the river pilot off Gravesend, all within the space of the early hours, *Enterprise* had berthed at Purfleet's floating link-span in the glare of morning sunlight. During breakfast, all the noise and bustle of the turnround had begun. The scene was little different to that described at the other ports of call over the past week.

Arrival at Purfleet.
Here the ship was moored to a Thames-side floating pontoon that was served with freight via a link-span bridge.

For me it was time to leave. Disappointed not to be completing the circuit with the ship along the East Coast to Hull but glad of the near 3,000 miles behind, from which I had gleaned so much. All too soon, amidst fleeting farewells to Captain and crew, and with visits from Customs and Immigration Officers, the taxi that I was to share into town with the Turnbulls had arrived. Such was the hubbub around the ship and shore that our departure went almost unnoticed. The irony was that on taking a last glance to the ship through the taxi's rear window I was not to know that I was to see her again the following day.

While wedged in a corner of the Hull-bound Inter-City, I suddenly remembered my tape recorder. A quick search through my baggage confirmed my fears. Through the hurried departure I had overlooked a final check through my cabin. The recorder had been packed in a dressing table drawer for safety during the gale – it had not been used since. Instinctively I contacted the ship from a public phone on arrival at Hull's Paragon Station. Within minutes the item had been found and at John Garvey's suggestion it was to be brought from Purfleet to Hull on the ship and handed to the shore office. It would remain there until such time as I could collect it.

The following day, having grudgingly made a hasty return to work, I sneaked an early evening, thirty-mile drive to Queen Elizabeth Dock. On arrival the scene was much the same as on the day I had embarked. The Rotterdam-bound ferry *Norland* was again entering the Humber from the lock. Following, a re-bunkered and stored *Baltic Enterprise* was scribing an arc in the dock water. She had hauled north from Purfleet overnight, turned round near capacity freight decks and was now making her routine burdened exit for Helsinki and Kotka.

I quickly collected the stray recorder from the dockside office and made for the lock pit in time to see *Enterprise* make her departure. There were new faces among the mooring deck crews and high up on the bridge wing – Gerry Brazendale had been relieved of his charge at Purfleet, the others had changed over at Hull.

With all the usual care and precision the *Baltic Enterprise* was duly locked through to the river. The dockmaster's whistle gave the all clear and her propellers bit furiously at the murky Humber. Her bow was swung round to head for the sea and another voyage had begun – yet another chapter in her log – it was **Ro-Ro to the Baltic** all over once more.

Epilogue

The voyage described took place in the summer of 1979. The text aims to cover situations, sightings and timings as accurately as possible. Naturally the subsequent years have seen a progression of changes and developments, not only in the maritime world but to the political map of Eastern Europe. The reader will be well aware of the German reunification and the break up of the Soviet Union twelve years onwards of the story; however the follow-on career of the *Baltic Enterprise* and some selected features of the narration which have been subjected to change are updated below.

M.V. BALTIC ENTERPRISE
The *Baltic Enterprise* was completed as yard no. 209 in June 1973 at Rauma-Repola, Rauma, Finland, (later to become Aker Yards Oy. then STX Finland Oy.) From delivery to the United Baltic Corporation mid-summer 1973 the *Baltic Enterprise* operated on the Finanglia U.K./Finland services for ten consecutive years. She was then sold to Losinjki Plovidba, Rijcka, Croatia in 1983 and renamed the M.V. *Lipa*. After twenty-five years operating throughout the Mediterranean and northern Europe she was regarded by the Croatians as one of the most legendary of ships. In the summer of 2008 the *Lipa* made her last voyage – to be broken up on the beaches of Alang, India.

Throughout the text the measurements of the ship are stated as imperial. In today's metric world the basics read: length – 135.5 metres; breadth – 22.3 metres; draught – 6.6 metres; lane metres – 1,270m. Her gross tonnage is quoted as 4,667. This is a volume measure of enclosed space rather than weight. This is based on the formula of 100 cubic feet = one gross ton. Up to 1982 the enclosed volume of car/freight decks aboard ferries was not included. Vessels laid down after that date are measured by an updated system which includes the volume of all enclosed vehicle space. Later in her career the ship was measured under the revised rules and re-registered at 12,110gt. Her deadweight tonnage remained at 5,710dwt.

UNITED BALTIC CORPORATION
U.B.C. replaced the *Baltic Enterprise* and *Baltic Progress* with a new generation of ro-ro vessels – the *Baltic Eagle* and *Baltic Eider*. Consequently the formers' personnel were progressively redeployed aboard the newer vessels. In 2005 the United Baltic Corporation went out of business when its parent company, Andrew Weir Shipping, sold its fleet to fund new buildings for M.O.D. service.

M.V. NORLAND (chapters 1,2,14)
After completion by yards of A.G. Weser, Bremerhaven for North Sea Ferries in June 1974 the *Norland* entered service on the established overnight Hull/Europoort (Rotterdam) service. In April 1982 the *Norland* was requisitioned by the M.O.D. for deployment as a troopship. She sailed 8,000 miles directly into the Falkland Island hostilities with 900 paratroopers aboard. After ten months of monumental service in the South Atlantic the *Norland* returned to her home port of Hull. She was lengthened in 1987 and remained ferrying the North Sea between Hull and Zeebrugge until being sold in 2002 to SNAV of Italy. As the *SNAV Sicilia* she spent the rest of her days sailing overnight between Naples and Palermo. The *SNAV Sicilia* (ex-*Norland)* was sold for breaking in 2010.

M.V. TOR ANGLIA (chapter 3)
Following ten years of North Sea service the 1966-built *Tor Anglia* was sold to Mediterranean interests, sailing out of Italy as the *Expresso Olbia.* During the early 1980s she was chartered to TT Line operating in the Baltic as the *Robin Hood II.* In 1983 she was sold to Sardinia Ferries to become *Sardinia Nova* and later named *Baia Sardinia.* After various charters, which again brought her back to northern Europe onwards of 1990, the former *Tor Anglia* was finally broken up at Aliaga, Turkey in 2010.

G.T.S. FINNJET (chapter 6)
The *Finnjet* was built for Finnlines in 1977 to operate between Helsinki and Travemünde, Germany, replacing several other vessels. Her exceptionally fast speed was achieved by the use of fuel-hungry gas turbine engines. During the winter 1981/82 she was additionally equipped with more economical diesel engines for use during periods

when traffic did not justify the speed required to make as many Baltic crossings per week. In 1986 the *Finnjet* was acquired by EFFOA continuing her trans-Baltic services which later included Tallinn, Rostock and St Petersburg. In spring 2005, under the ownership of Sea Containers, she was chartered to replace accommodation destroyed by Hurricane Katrina and moored at Baton Rouge, Louisiana USA. In 2008 *Finnjet* was sold to Sea Club of the Netherlands and renamed the *DA Vincini* but later sold to the breakers.

THE HUMBER BRIDGE (chapter 2)
The bridge was first opened to traffic on 24th June 1981 and officially opened by H.M. The Queen on 17th July of that year. At 4,626 feet (1,410 metres) and with a total length of 7,283 feet (2,220 metres) the Humber Bridge was the longest single-span in the world for sixteen years until the opening of the Great Belt Bridge, Denmark, in 1997.

SPURN HEAD (chapter 3)
The Humber Lifeboat continues to be the only R.N.L.I. craft manned by a full time crew. However onwards of 2012 the crew's families were no longer housed there. This being the outcome of increasingly high tides eroding the connecting road along the three-mile pencil spit of land that linked their remote homes with essential services. Spurn Lighthouse was in use from 1895 until it was decommissioned in 1985.

THE ORESUND BRIDGE / DROGDEN TUNNEL (chapter 6)
A fixed link for both road and rail between Sweden and Denmark was completed on 14th August 1999. This being achieved by linking the Swedish shore near Malmö by a 5-mile long bridge to an artificial island named Peberholm. Then a 2.5-mile tunnel under the Drogden Channel connects with the Danish island of Amager which is also the site of Copenhagen's Kastrup Airport. The Oresund Bridge is the longest combined road/rail bridge in Europe. This development did not affect shipping travelling to and from the Baltic Sea via the Drogden Channel.

FERRIES FROM HELSINKI (chapter 8)
After the collapse of the Soviet Union in 1991 regular ferry services out of Helsinki extended. Added to the long established ferry links with Stockholm, Sweden and Germany were frequent services to: Tallinn, Estonia; St Petersburg, Russia; and Gdynia, Poland.

MÄNTYLUOTO – OIL RIG CONSTRUCTION (chapter 10)
The production/maintenance of oil rigs/platforms at Mäntyluoto came to an end with a view to the construction of the Great Belt Bridge. Built between 1991 and 1998 the East Bridge spanning the Danish 'Great Belt Channel' allowed a maximum vertical clearance of 65metres (213 feet) for shipping. Having height far in excess of this clearance and being the only route the 'rigs' could transit between the Baltic and the rest of the world's seas meant that it was no longer an industry that could continue. In 1991 Finland sued Denmark at the International Court of Justice because of this. The two countries negotiated a financial compensation and Finland withdrew the lawsuit.

BALTIC ICE (chapter 11)
Following his wish to return to the Baltic Sea to experience winter conditions the author sailed aboard the *Baltic Eagle* (*Enterprise*'s successor) in February 1986. Voyaging north to Helsinki and Kotka the ship followed countless miles of ice strewn passages. Though not as severe as described in chapter 11 the sub zero conditions produced an indelible encounter.

THE KIEL CANAL (chapter 12)
The Kiel Canal remains much as described. Carrying upwards of 35,000 vessels annually it continues to be the busiest sea-linking waterway in the world. Height restrictions at its bridges however dismiss its use by the escalating number of cruise ships destined for the Baltic. The 21st century has seen these vessels increase in size beyond all expectations leaving the 'Great Belt' transit as the only option for the popular 'Baltic Capitals' cruises. Some mid-sized cruise ships have had upper-works modifications which enables them to transit the canal but, at the time of writing, the building of 100,000gt plus, 'tower block' giants appears to be the way forward with all major cruise ship operators.

The 5 710 tonne d.w. "Baltic Enterprise", fourth vessel in a series of five ordered from Rauma Repola Oy, of Finland, for service between Finland and the U.K. A notable feature of these vessels is the twin stern door arrangement which forms loading ramps for two-way wheeled traffic.

'Baltic Enterprise' — first U.K.-owned vessel built in Finland

BY THE end of 1973, the Finnish shipbuilder, Rauma Repola Oy, of Rauma will have delivered the last ship in a series of five 18-knot, 5 710 tonne d.w. roll-on/roll-off cargo vessels specially designed for a rapid cargo service between the U.K. and Finland. The first three vessels, "Antares", "Orion" and "Sirius", are now in service on this route for the Finland Steamship Co., while the fourth ship, "Baltic Enterprise", recently joined this service but is owned by the British company, United Baltic Corporation Ltd. (UBC). The last vessel, to be delivered by the end of this year, will join the "Baltic Enterprise" on a new UBC service from Purfleet, England, to Finland.

Built to Lloyd's Register ✠ 100 A1, LMC and UMS classes, and Finnish ice class 1A standard, the "Baltic Enterprise" is understood to be the first ship built in Finland for a British owner

PRINCIPAL PARTICULARS "BALTIC ENTERPRISE"	
	metres
Length, o.a.	137·50
Length, b.p.	126·50
Breadth, moulded	22·30
Depth, to main deck	11·50
Draught	6·64
Deadweight	5 710 tonnes
Cargo capacity, bale	20 386 m³
Machinery	2 × Stork-Werkspoor 9TM410
Output	2 × 5 250 bhp at 530 rev/min
Speed, service	18 knots

and has a broad transom stern which accommodates two 6·6 m wide by 6·2 m high stern doors. These doors have been dimensioned to allow two-way traffic of wheeled vehicles through both simultaneously and, inside the vessel, stowage is arranged on three decks while space is also available on the weather deck. Access for vehicles to the upper 'tweendeck is by two Navire articulated ramps which are double hinged to enable them to be stowed beneath the weather deck when not in use, while direct access to the lower 'tweendeck is by a built-in downward slope arranged at the stern end of this deck.

Lift access to lower hold

Vehicles to be stowed in the lower hold at tank top level are lowered by a pair of MacGregor 40-ton lifts which take 45 seconds to move from the lower 'tweendeck to the tank top. Private cars can be driven from the upper 'tweendeck to the main deck by a ramp hinged from the main deck. The ship has a capacity for about 1 000 cars though fewer than this is normally carried to allow for a mixed cargo of containers, pallets, trailers, and cars.

Sixty 20-ft containers can be carried on the main deck and for handling these, a 20-ton Kone gantry crane is used to lift the containers from trailers on the 'tweendeck below, through twin MacGregor hatches on the deck, to the stowage positions. The crane has a hoisting speed of 25 m/min and the containers are stacked two high on the main deck. This arrangement of internal ramps and lifts, and the unloading of containers from trailers within the ship through hatchways to the main deck, as

The main deck of the "Baltic Enterprise" has at its forward end a CO₂ fire fighting installation and, amidships, twin vehicle access ramps to the 'tweendeck below.

COMPLEMENT	
Captain	Chief steward
Chief officer	Assistant steward (3)
Second officer	Chief cook
Third officer	Assistant cook
W.T. operator	Cook's boy
Chief engineer	Bosun
Second engineer	Seamen (6)
Third engineer	Greasers (2)
Fourth engineer	Passengers (12)
Electrician	

THE MOTOR SHIP

A view of the dining saloon, on the inboard bulkhead is an attractive mural of a nautical theme.

The wheelhouse interior showing the forward control console, twin Raytheon radar sets, and the free-standing helm.

well as the twin stern door arrangements, provides a very rapid cargo handling arrangement.

Medium-speed machinery installation

As normal practice with roll-on/roll-off vessels having a low engine-room headroom, medium-speed diesel engines are installed in the "Baltic Enterprise"; in this case two in-line Stork-Werkspoor 9TM410 engines of 5 250 bhp each. Each engine drives, through a Tacke reduction gear and Fawick Geislinger flexible coupling, a Kamewa c.p. propeller turning at 200 rev/min to provide the ship with a service speed of 18 knots. The main engines can be pneumatically controlled from the machinery control room and the propeller speed and pitch are further controlled by Combinator units in the wheelhouse which include Kamewa load control units to automatically set the propeller pitch and maintain the desired engine load conditions. To meet the Lloyd's Register UMS requirements, a Saab-Scania combined on/off and analogue alarm system is provided to monitor and protect the engine-room machinery.

For auxiliary purposes, three Stromberg alternators each of 660 kVA output and driven by Wärtsilä diesel engines provide a 380 volt, 50 cycle electrical supply. These are located in a separate auxiliary engine-room and at sea, normally one generator set provides the power requirements. Two Uudenkaupungin Telakka Unex oil-fired auxiliary boilers and one Svenska Maskinverken exhaust gas boiler provide the vessel's steam supply.

A 500 m³/h heeling pump is remote controlled from the engine-room or a deck cargo control office. The heeling pump, when on automatic control, is able to keep the ship on a constant even keel during cargo loading and discharge.

Navigation equipment installed in the wheelhouse includes Raytheon radars, a Plath direction finder, Sirius gyro compass, Arkas autopilot, Sal log, and Simrad echo sounder. Kelvin Hughes has supplied the radio installation and a fire detecting system has been provided by Salwico-Stromberg while a Ginge low-pressure CO_2 fire-fighting installation is placed in a forward deckhouse for protection of the 'tweendeck cargo spaces.

Article published in 'The Motor Ship', October 1973.

. . . .

The 1:100 scale builders' model of the *Baltic Enterprise* fortunately perpetuates the style and calibre of a state-of-the-art vessel from the early years of the dedicated roll-on roll-off freight ferry. (National Maritime Museum.)

FAREWELL TO THE BALTIC ENTERPRISE...

While in her last throes under the UBC house flag the ship completed a short charter to North Sea Ferries on the Hull<>Europoort service. She is seen here in early 1983 at the NSF Europoort (Rotterdam) terminal. (Cees de Bijl.)

Taking on bunkers at her Queen Elizabeth Dock, Hull berth the *Baltic Enterprise* is pictured shortly before her 1983 sale to Croatian interests.

Final glance - issuing a plume of exhaust smoke as in salute the *Baltic Enterprise* takes her leave from the Thames. Under new ownership she was renamed the *Lipa* and over a further 25 years sailed extensively for the Losinjplov and Valfract Lines in the Adriatic and Mediterranean Seas. She ultimately became regarded by the Croatians as

...'ONE OF THE MOST LEGENDARY OF SHIPS'.

***

Acknowledgements

Initially I am indebted to the foresight and help extended by senior management of the United Baltic Corporation. At all times my requests for information and access to M.V. *Baltic Enterprise* were met with their fullest co-operation. Without assistance of this nature there would have been no book.

Equally I am indebted to all the seagoing and shore staff of U.B.C. who consciously or unconsciously have contributed to this work. Several are mentioned within the text but there are many more that have made important contributions. It would be difficult to individually name each and every person who offered a wealth of information. I express my sincere thanks to all.

I would, however, take the opportunity to individually thank Captain Gerald Brazendale for his cooperation both at sea and ashore, not least reading through the manuscript and giving invaluable advice.

Further my gratitude for help received extends to: Humber Pilot John Ashby; Ms Jane Ashford, Dunelm Public Relations Ltd.; The Docks Manager, Associated British Ports, Hull; Captain Claes Soderholm, Finland Steamship Company; The National Maritime Museum, Greenwich. And sincere thanks to Susan Hutchinson of Lodge Books for her invaluable help and advice in the publication of this book.

Last but by no means least my warmest thanks go to my wife Mollie for her forbearance and support while I was preoccupied in compiling this book.

BIBLIOGRAPHY
Scandinavia by W. R. Mead and Wendy Hall
Finland by Gladys Nichol
Gotland by Arthur Spencer
Supership by Noel Mostert
Steamship by T. F. Wickham
Lighthouses of England and Wales by Derrick Jackson
Kotka by Jukka Vehkasalo
The Hull Daily Mail
City of Kingston upon Hull by W. R. Watkinson

Lightning Source UK Ltd.
Milton Keynes UK
UKHW010859091221
395376UK00011B/1378